A CIVILIAN RESPONSE TO
ETHNO-RELIGIOUS CONFLICT

A CIVILIAN RESPONSE TO ETHNO-RELIGIOUS CONFLICT

The Gülen Movement in Southeast Turkey

Mehmet Kalyoncu

The Light

New Jersey

Published by The Light, Inc.
26 Worlds Fair Dr. Unit C
Somerset, New Jersey, 08873, USA

www.thelightpublishing.com

Library of Congress Cataloging-in-Publication Data

Kalyoncu, Mehmet.
 A civilian response to ethno-religious conflict : the Gulen movement in southeast Turkey / Mehmet Kalyoncu.
    p. cm.
 Includes bibliographical references and index.
 ISBN-13: 978-1-59784-025-5 (pbk.)
 1.   Turkey--Ethnic relations. 2.   Gülen, Fethullah. 3.   Islam--Turkey--Mardin. 4. Mardin (Turkey)--Ethnic relations. I. Title.
 DR434.K34 2007
 297.6'5095667--dc22

                                     2007027640

Printed by
Çağlayan A.Ş., Izmir - Turkey

CONTENTS

PREFACE

The fundamental question that inspired the research for this book was the following: What enables the Gülen movement, originally a Turkish-Muslim social movement, to reach out to communities across the world that are socially, economically, and politically quite different from one another, and to function in all of them almost equally successfully? Movement participants have established educational institutions, schools or cultural centers, in more than ninety countries. What is it about the movement that appeals to the local people in those countries? Is it something to do with what movement volunteers provide in practice in the communities where they are present, or with the way they relate to local people, or with the socio-economic and political context of the communities where movement participants live and work?

It was a challenge to make generalizations about the Gülen movement, which has active volunteers in more than ninety countries and more than five hundred institutions. It was not feasible to conduct research in all or most of the countries where the movement has emerged. What came to my aid for this study was a city which reflected many aspects of the vast area across which the movement has emerged. The city of Mardin as a case study may not suffice to make overarching generalizations about the Gülen movement. Nevertheless, it comes close to serving such attempts well, given its characteristic ethno-religious diversity and the socio-economic and political problems it has suffered. The analysis of the Gülen movement in Mardin, how the local people of different ethno-religious backgrounds mobilized and participated, how this eased the ethno-religious tensions, and how the work of volunteers minimized the popular support for the terrorist organizations such as the PKK and Hizbullah,[1] hint at ways to understand the appeal of Gülen's and the movement's ideas to people of different ethno-religious backgrounds. The success of movement participants in Mardin also lays out possible guidelines for tackling ethno-religious conflicts elsewhere across the world.

Mardin is a city on Turkey's border with Syria. The locals call it the city of seven languages and seven religions. The city has a diverse population that includes Turks, Kurds, Arabs, Yezidi, and Assyrian Christians, as well as the subgroups of Assyrian Christianity, such as Chaldeans and Syrian Jacobites. The city also had a sizeable Jewish community until the 1950s: most of the Mardinian Jews migrated to Israel after 1948 for a new beginning.

What made Mardin most attractive as a case study for this research was the city's resemblance to the majority of the regions across the world which suffer ethno-religious conflicts. Despite the fact that the various religious and ethnic groups have lived in Mardin for centuries relatively peacefully, in the last two decades ethno-religious differences have been exploited by terrorist organizations such as the PKK (Kurdistan Workers Party) and Hizbullah to garner popular support for their causes. As a result of the extensive presence of terrorist organizations in the city, Mardin topped the list of the cities for many Turks to stay away from.

The methodology of this research included both the use of interviews as a primary source of data and an analysis of the literature of and about the Gülen movement. The secondary sources of data were more or less the same literature upon which earlier studies on the Gülen movement have built. What distinguishes this study from its earlier counterparts is its heavy emphasis on interviews with local people and its drawing conclusions on the actual work carried out by the Gülen movement volunteers in Mardin.

It may be difficult to argue that the local people's opinions, desires, and concerns are identical to those of all people who suffer similar problems stemming from a prolonged ethno-religious conflict. Nevertheless, identifying those opinions, desires, and concerns may help us to understand communities suffering similar problems elsewhere in the world. Unfortunately, it is not difficult to find such regions across the world. The most notable of such regions are Palestine, where it appears that all possible political solutions proposed to solve the Arab-Israeli conflict have failed, and Iraq, where the never-ending conflicts along the fault-lines of Kurdish–Arab and Sunni–Shiite identities plague the fate of the country. In fact, the example put forth by the educational campaign by Gülen movement volunteers a couple of hundred miles north could provide a sustainable solution to the ethno-religious conflicts both in Iraq and Palestine.

Despite its global reach, the Gülen movement has not been studied extensively by scholars. The limited amount of academic literature addresses such topics as Fethullah Gülen himself, in his capacity as an Islamic scholar, reformer, and educator, as well as the schools opened by Gülen movement participants. Little attention, however, has been paid to the diffusion of the movement into a wide range of different societies in a relatively short time.

This book attempts to explain how the movement has arisen and attained a global outreach. In chapter 1, I outline its beginnings. In chapter 2, I review the existing literature about the Gülen movement and indicate the absence of scholarly work dealing with the movement's practical aspects in general and with its diffusion mechanism in particular. Chapter 3 seeks to identify the key concepts of its discourse, the discourse that has propelled individuals to participate in its activities. This chapter also looks at two sorts of concepts: theoretical and operational/structural. Theoretical concepts are derived from Gülen's speeches and writings and are the most frequently repeated concepts that seem to motivate the participants in the movement. Operational and structural concepts are simply the activities that are carried out in a relatively organized fashion by the participants, and hence constitute the daily practices inspired by the theoretical concepts of this discourse.

Chapter 4 analyzes the beginnings of the Gülen movement in Mardin, a major city in southeastern Turkey. It looks at the movement's emergence and historical development in the city, how movement activists first contacted local Mardinians, and how those Mardinians have in turn mobilized as a result of the inspiration and educational paradigm offered by Gülen and the other participants in the Gülen movement. Chapter 5 examines the specific institutions that came into being as the Gülen movement took root in Mardin, their activities, how they interact with the local Mardinians, and what they mean for the local people. The final chapter attempts to show how the mechanism of the movement can explain its successful outreach into many different communities across the world.

ACKNOWLEDGMENTS

This book evolved out of the research and writing of the master's thesis which I submitted to Georgetown University's Graduate School of Arts and Sciences while completing my graduate studies at the Center for Eurasian, Russian and East European Studies of the Edmund A. Walsh School of Foreign Service. I would like to thank my thesis advisors, Dr. Charles King and Dr. Jennifer Long, who guided me through the research and writing of this thesis, and Dr. Sylvia Onder, from whose scholarship I benefited deeply. I am also grateful to Georgetown University's School of Foreign Service for the research opportunities it provided to me.

The book might have gone unwritten without the encouragement of many friends and colleagues who were enthusiastic to read the findings of my research in this form. The list of those people who did not spare their encouragement throughout the preparation of this book for publication is quite long. I would like to express my particular gratitude to Dr. Alp Aslandoğan and Muhammed Çetin who gave their time and invaluable insights on presenting my research as a book to a global audience.

Finally, I would like to thank all my interviewees in Mardin and other cities in Turkey as well as those in the United States without whose candid responses and generous time this book would not have been possible.

1

Gülen and the
Origins of the Movement

The Gülen movement is a faith-based civil society movement which initially comprised mostly a loose network of
individual pious Muslims and is currently active in some
ninety-one countries. Throughout the years it has come to
include secular Muslims, as well as non-Muslims.

The movement emerged in the late 1960s in Turkey with
a handful of people who were attracted by an influential preacher and Islamic scholar, M. Fethullah Gülen (1941–), and his
circle of admirers has expanded ever since. Gülen, a state-
authorized mosque preacher, delivered sermons in major cities
in Turkey until 1992. The mosque congregations present at
his sermons averaged from four to five thousand people at a
time, and many more who have not attended have listened to
Gülen's speeches in recorded form. In this period, Gülen
also spoke and gave seminars in many secular settings, such
as halls and cafes.

In contrast to an ordinary mosque preacher that focuses
exclusively on religious matters and texts, Gülen has spoken
and written prolifically about a variety of subjects that, according to many, might seem beyond the ordinary subject matter

of most preachers. The most notable of these subjects have included the Qur'an and science, social justice, human rights, the metaphysical world, thoughts on economics, child education, parenthood and parents' rights, in addition to many other more standard religious subjects such as the interpretation of the Qur'an and the sayings of the Prophet Muhammad.[2] Gülen's knowledge of the specifics of the subjects he speaks about and his frequent references to such Western luminaries as Goethe, Dostoyevsky, Tolstoy, Jacques Cousteau, Newton, Pascal, and Einstein, distinguish him from his contemporaries and have enabled him to appeal to a broader audience beyond mosque-goers.

In mosque congregations and public conferences of the 1970s and 1980s, Gülen's listeners comprised mostly low- to middle-income businessmen, with a small number of wealthy ones, and university students who would soon be, respectively, sponsors of and teachers in the Gülen-inspired educational institutions and cultural centers. Inspired by Gülen's frequent emphasis on reconciling moral values and religion with modern science and on opening schools where the students could receive a modern education, including science, without neglecting moral values and standards, one group opened the first university preparatory course in Izmir, by far the most secular city in western Turkey, in 1979. Hundreds of university preparatory courses have followed since then. In the early 1980s, Prime Minister Turgut Özal instigated a number of liberalization and privatization policies. Gülen movement participants used those legal spaces and opportunities wisely to consolidate their provision of educational and cultural activities and services.

In 1982, groups of people inspired by Gülen's educational paradigm opened their first two private secondary high schools in Izmir and Istanbul. These were soon followed by another one in Ankara. As well as teaching arts and humanities, compared to their public counterparts and other private schools, the Gülen-inspired schools have been extremely successful in preparing students for university admissions tests and for national and international science contests in math, physics, chemistry, biology, and computer science. The success of the university preparatory courses and private schools established by the movement was, for many, a confirmation of what Gülen had always argued in his speeches and writings: that one could be a pious Muslim and yet modern at the same time, for modernity and Islam are not mutually exclusive; rather, they are complementary. As the number of Gülen-inspired educational institutions increased, the size and influence of the movement grew. Therefore, the 1970s and 1980s were years during which the Gülen movement achieved broader public recognition, expanded its base, and gained a foothold in the field of education.

The collapse of the Soviet Union in 1991 and the independence of the Turkic republics in both Central Asia and the Caucasus provided opportunities for educational projects in the Gülen movement to become transnational. With schools in Turkey, the participants in the movement had already developed the capacity to expand outreach and to open schools in the newly independent Turkic republics. In his sermons in the late 1980s, Gülen increasingly advised his audiences to prepare to help the countries with shared cultural values and history which had suffered under the communist regime of the Soviet Union to develop their human capital, since the federation was soon to collapse and this would allow the Turkic republics within it to become independent.

Once the Soviet Union had collapsed, a group of individuals comprising teachers and businessmen inspired by Gülen's education vision opened the first high school abroad in Azerbaijan in 1992. In the same year, the first Gülen-inspired school was opened in Kazakhstan and, in the following two years, a further twenty-eight schools were opened in that country.[3] In 1996, participants in the movement for the first time opened a university in Kazakhstan. Between 1992 and 1994, schools were opened in Kyrgyzstan, where participants now run twelve high schools and one university. Simultaneously, some twenty schools were opened in Turkmenistan. In Uzbekistan on the other hand, the movement has experienced difficulties, despite some early successes. Although eighteen schools were opened there between 1992 and 1995, due to a diplomatic crisis that broke out between Turkey and Uzbekistan, all Turkish-initiated institutions were closed, including the schools.

The movement did not limit its scope to the Turkic republics. During the same period, starting in the early 1990s, the volunteers of the movement opened similar schools in various non-Muslim countries in Eastern Europe and the former Soviet Union, such as Bulgaria, Romania, Moldova, Ukraine, and Georgia, and reached out to such Asia-Pacific countries as the Philippines, Cambodia, Australia, Indonesia, Thailand, Vietnam, Malaysia, South Korea, and Japan.

Starting in the mid-1990s, the Gülen movement moved into yet another field of social life in Turkey. In 1994, the Journalists and Writers Foundation, a non-governmental organization promoting intercultural dialogue (and of which

Fethullah Gülen is the honorary president), convened members of different faiths in Turkey in a public event featuring renowned intellectuals, public figures, and politicians. This event was the first of its kind ever in Turkish history, and the fact that it was organized by a movement perceived as Islamic was also a surprise to many. The following years witnessed similar interfaith activities, such as panels, conferences, and other public events. Gülen's visit and private audience with Pope John Paul II in 1998 was a ground-breaking event for Muslim-Christian relations in Turkey. Yet, hard-line secular and marginal Islamic groups in Turkey criticized him severely for it. The first group argued that such a meeting was a sign that Gülen had aspirations to create his own Islamic state on the model of the Vatican. The second group argued that Gülen's teachings and his movement were heretical, since his visit with the Pope was, according to their interpretation of Islam, unacceptable.

Given the absence of the actual teaching of Islam as a religion in its overall activities and the nature of its activities, which mostly involve secular education, it is difficult to describe the Gülen movement phenomenon simply as a religious movement. In the countries in which the movement is active, the local media do not normally identify the movement as promoting Islam or as pursuing a religious agenda. However, it would be easy to describe it as a faith-based civic movement because of the mobilizing influence of Islam on individuals associated with it. Gülen himself, as a Turkish Islamic scholar, is a pious Muslim who reportedly strives to practice every tradition of the Prophet Muhammad in his own life and, accordingly, encourages others to do so as well. Many teachers in the Gülen-inspired schools in Turkey and abroad

The "dormatories"?

are pious Muslims who view their service in these schools as a way of serving God through serving their fellow humans.

The central puzzle about the Gülen movement is the seemingly contradictory relationship between its socio-cultural identity and its apparent success in reaching out to communities all over the world that are politically, economically, and culturally distinct from one another. In other words, a movement that has a Turkish Islamic identity would seem to face serious obstacles in its effort to expand into countries that are neither Turkic nor Islamic. Yet, the movement exists and is active in as many non-Muslim countries as in Muslim countries. The countries where Gülen movement volunteers are active include not only those with a Turkic and Muslim heritage, but also those with Christian, Buddhist, and Hindu traditions, and countries like Russia, which has historically been cautious of anything Islamic.[4]

How has this social and cultural movement become so successful in reaching out to very different communities and cultures? I seek to account for the extraordinary success of the Gülen movement by drawing on major theories of social mobilization and then integrating them with original fieldwork in the multi-ethnic environment of Mardin, an important regional city in southeastern Turkey where Gülen movement participants have been especially active. Although the thesis draws on only a single fieldwork case, it suggests that the diffusion of the Gülen movement into Mardin's multi-ethnic and multi-religious community provides a window into understanding its spread into very different communities on a global scale; that is, I have investigated the mechanism of diffusion of the movement, but I do not aim to evaluate the activities nor judge the impact of the movement on the societies in which it emerges. Rather, I seek to understand the relationships within the educational service projects that have allowed it to succeed.

The Gülen movement provides a unique example of a particular type of faith-based civil society initiative and thereby challenges mainstream ideas about Islamic mobilization. Islamic movements have often been perceived as being either Muslims' reaction against the West or caused by political and economic deprivations in their communities. Such Islamic movements include the Muslim Brotherhood of Egypt, the Hizb-ut Tahrir of Pakistan and Central Asia, and Hizbullah of Lebanon. The common feature of these movements is that they all utilize Islamic discourse to garner popular support, are composed exclusively of Muslims, and are, in general, reactionary or revolutionary. However, the Gülen movement started out utilizing Islamic discourse in its early stages in Turkey to garner popular support and, over time, has emphasized the secular and humanistic elements in its discourse such as quality education, empathic acceptance of others and universal ethical values as it has reached out to broader audiences. Although the movement has remained Islamic at an individual level, it is a secular social movement overall.

2

The Gülen Movement and
Diffusion Theory

Although Fethullah Gülen has been a prominent public fig-
ure since the late 1960s and the movement that has formed
around his ideas has been an important agent of change within Turkish society, he and the movement he has inspired have
attracted academic attention only in the last decade. Scholars
have focused on three dimensions of the Gülen movement's
activities: interfaith dialogue, Gülen's views on secularism and
the state, and education.

GÜLEN AND INTERFAITH DIALOGUE

Gülen and movement volunteers have sought to establish
dialogue among different segments of Turkish society, pri-
marily between secularists and the faithful, and secondarily
between Muslims and non-Muslims living in Turkey. The
Ramadan Dinner events held by the Journalists and Writers
Foundation in 1994 were the first of their kind in terms of
bringing together intellectuals, politicians, and other prominent figures who were believed to belong to different camps
and, hence, hold irreconcilable views. Such dialogue events

were followed by similar ones bringing together the representatives of Catholic, Orthodox Christian, Jewish, and Armenian communities in Turkey. Gülen's visit with Pope John Paul II in the Vatican in February 1998 was a highpoint for the development of interfaith dialogue in Turkey.

According to Sidney Griffith and Zeki Sarıtoprak, one result of Gülen's meeting with Pope John Paul II was that Gülen and his associates received wide public support in Turkey. At the same time, however, they were severely criticized by hard-line secularists and radical Islamists.[5] The first group criticized Gülen's initiative on the basis that such a meeting required the state's permission and that Gülen, by speaking to the Pope on his own behalf to promote interfaith dialogue, had signaled his desire to create an Islamic state with himself as head. The second group criticized Gülen for degrading Islam by engaging in dialogue with a non-Muslim leader. Griffith and Sarıtoprak contend that the idea of interfaith dialogue pioneered by Gülen in Turkey is rooted in his interpretation of Islamic principles and Qur'anic verses, most notably the *basmala,* the phrase recurrent at the beginning of all but one of the Qur'an's *surahs*.[6] The phrase describes God as "the Compassionate and the Merciful." Repeating this phrase one hundred and thirteen times, the Qur'an teaches Muslims to be compassionate and merciful in their relations with their fellow human beings and with nature.

Moreover, Griffith and Sarıtoprak argue that Gülen's interfaith dialogue efforts stem from his perspectives on Islam's ecumenical aspect. In other words, Islam not only accepts the central role of such figures as Moses and Jesus, but also requires good Muslims to incorporate the teachings of these figures as part of their own faith. Similarly, for Gülen, not to believe in

• Freewill vs. determin is mistaken thought.
• It is actually simple determin vs. complex determin

the Biblical prophets mentioned in the Qur'an is enough of a reason to place someone outside the circle of Islam.[7] Along the same lines as Griffith and Sarıtoprak, Kurtz maintains that Gülen advocates tolerance toward and dialogue with others because of his commitment to Islam. According to Kurtz, the pillars of Gülen's method of dialogue comprise love, compassion, tolerance, and forgiveness, all of which Gülen derives from Qur'anic teachings.[8]

GÜLEN AND THE MIDDLE WAY

The wide publicity that Gülen and the movement gained throughout the 1990s also brought his views on modernity, secularism, and other contemporary debates under scholarly scrutiny. Kuru considers Gülen a moderate with regard to the ongoing debate about the compatibility between Islam and modernity. Kuru suggests that extreme modernists and religious fundamentalists ironically agree that the four features of modernity (modern science, rationalism, the idea of progress, and individual free will) are incompatible with the four aspects of Muslim tradition (Islamic knowledge, revelation, a conservative understanding of time, and the belief in destiny).[9] In contrast, he argues, Gülen denies such an incompatibility, seeing it as a false dichotomy, and takes a moderate position.[10] Gülen contends that "Islam, being the 'middle way' of absolute balance—balance between materialism and spiritualism, between rationalism and mysticism, between worldliness and excessive asceticism, between this world and the next—and inclusive of the ways of all the previous prophets, makes a choice according to the situation."[11]

Along similar lines to Kuru, Thomas Michel argues that Gülen's criticism of both traditional and modern secular education systems illustrates his quest for a middle path between modernity and tradition. Michel suggests that Gülen's criticism of the *madrasa*s and the *takya*s (traditional Islamic institutions of education) rests precisely on the grounds that they do not meet the demands of modern life as they lack the methods and tools for preparing students to make positive contributions to the modern world because of their failure to integrate science and technology into their traditional curriculums. However, Gülen criticizes modern secular schools for failing to convey spiritual and ethical values to students, even if they might be able to teach scientific knowledge and technical skills. To resolve this, Gülen proposes an education system that integrates scientific knowledge and ethical values.[12] In this vein, Nilüfer Göle suggests that Gülen's integrated approach enables people to preserve what is best and still valuable from the past as well as to accept and make use of scientific and technological advances, whereas isolationist approaches have been divisive and have polarized society into secular versus Islamic, modern versus traditional, and scientific versus religious camps.[13]

Regarding the relationship between science and religion, Gülen seems to seek the middle way as well. Osman Bakar suggests that Gülen finds the two not contradictory but complementary.[14] Gülen first distinguishes between absolute truth and relative truth, which religion and science, respectively, seek. According to Gülen, "Truth is not something the human mind produces. Truth exists independently of man and man's task is to seek it."[15] Moreover, while religion represents those absolute truths that are about the essence of the universe and have existed since the creation of the universe, science represents relative truths produced to help humanity understand those absolute truths. Gülen views religion and science as not genuinely in conflict, since the latter depends on empirical data and their rational—yet relative— interpretation by humans with limited knowledge.[16]

GÜLEN AND EDUCATION

Along with his unusual views on modernity, secularism, and science, Gülen's views on education have also been studied by scholars. Thomas Michel defines Gülen's educational vision as integrating the insights and strengths found in the various education systems of the past and the present and as bringing about a "marriage of mind and heart" in order to raise individuals of "thought, action, and inspiration."[17] According to Michel, Gülen envisions an education system that would not only teach students marketable skills, but also educate them to have ideals:

> Gülen's main interest in education is the future. He wants to form reformers—that is, those who, fortified with a value system that takes into account both the physical and non-material aspects of humankind, can conceive and bring about the needed changes in society.[18]

However, Bekim Agai considers Gülen's vision of education to be limited to the Muslim world. He claims that Gülen aspires to use modern education to stop what he sees as a process of decline in the Muslim world. He wants to create an educated elite within the Islamic *umma* (community) in general and within the Turkish nation in particular.[19] In addition, Berna Turam suggests that the Gülen movement seeks to reconcile Islamic culture and identity with a secular regime by adopting modern educational techniques and putting them into practice in its schools.[20] It can be noted, however, that the ideas of these two writers do not appear to account fully for the range of activities of Gülen movement volunteers in non-Muslim and non-Turkic countries and communities.

DIFFUSION OF SOCIAL MOVEMENTS

Most studies of the Gülen movement have focused on the personality of Gülen himself. The movement has been explained by examining Gülen's own views on modernity, science, and secularism. As a result, scholars have generally ignored the precise mechanisms of diffusion of the movement and have not linked the movement to existing theories of social mobilization. The following section analyzes those key concepts from social mobilization theory that can provide insight into the successes of the Gülen movement.

Doug McAdam and Dieter Rucht argue that two theories, resource mobilization theory and political process theory, have dominated the literature on social movements. However, they contend, less attention has been paid to intra- and inter-movement relations as a means of spreading. Therefore, they have developed a model of cross-national diffusion of ideas within social movements that emphasizes both the role of interpersonal relations in encouraging an initial identification of activist-adopters in one country with activist-transmitters in another, as well as the role of non-relational channels as the principal means of information transmission once the initial identification is established.[21]

Differing from those mainstream diffusion theorists who define diffusion as the spread of innovation, McAdam and Rucht perceive the concept of diffusion, in more general terms, as the spread of ideas and practices. They suggest that diffusion processes have so far been studied in such areas as the spread of language, consumer goods, technology, and techniques,[22] but have not been examined in terms of the spread of social movements. In order to apply diffusion theory to social movements, McAdam and Rucht define diffusion in more general terms as "the acceptance of some specific item, over time, by adopting units—individuals, groups, communities—that are linked both to external channels of communication and to each other by means of both a structure of social relations and a system of values, or culture."[23] According to this definition, diffusion consists of four essential components: first, a person, group or organization that serves as the emitter or transmitter; second, a person, group or organization that is the adopter; third, the item that is diffused, such as material goods, information, skills, and the like; and fourth, a channel of diffusion that may consist of persons or media that link the transmitter and the adopter.

In their model, McAdam and Rucht pay special attention to the channel of diffusion. They note that, depending on the channel, there are two models: relational and non-relational. The relational model is a traditional perspective on diffusion, one marked by interpersonal contact between transmitters and adopters. The non-relational model defines diffusion as being carried out through means other than direct personal contacts, such as the media and literature. As McAdam and Rucht note, the non-relational model was utilized first by David Strang and John Meyer to explain the uniformity of policy practices worldwide that could not be explained on the basis of direct personal contact among policymakers. Strang and Meyer concluded that "cross-national diffusion can occur in the absence of high levels of direct contact, provided non-relational channels of information are available to a group of potential adopters who define themselves as similar to the transmitters and the idea or item in question as relevant to their situation."[24] Taking their conclusion as the starting point, McAdam and Rucht apply this model to the study of social movements, specifically the interaction between the American and the German New Left.

How Does the Gülen Movement Diffuse?

The relational and non-relational models of diffusion both prove useful in explaining the spread of the Gülen movement. The relational model explains the spread of ideas, values, and vision through direct interpersonal contacts and relations, whereas the non-relational (indirect) model explains the spread through such non-relational channels as the media and literature. Nonetheless, to apply this diffusion theory to the spread of the Gülen movement, it must differ from its original formulation. McAdam and Rucht utilized the model to explain the interaction and congruity between social movements that are active in different national or transnational settings. The Gülen movement case introduces a new dimension to the model. Normally, the model assumes that both the transmitter and the adopter are equivalent actors, that is, person and person, group and group, or social movement and social movement. According to the model, a social movement that is active in one setting leads another movement that is active in another setting to adopt similar activities through its interpersonal relations with the latter and through non-relational channels from that point on. However, in the Gülen movement case, the movement originated in Turkey but went into different communities and made contact not with another social movement, but with individuals and social groups that are not necessarily engaged in collective action. In that sense, Gülen movement participants initiate activities in this new setting as local individuals and social groups mobilize toward realizing a shared vision of education.

The Gülen movement shows that both models, relational and non-relational, can operate simultaneously once interpersonal relations initiate the diffusion process. Before the movement participants launch educational and cultural activities in a new environment, be it a familiar or a completely strange community, they first and most importantly identify and make contact with local figures through personal visits. These local figures mostly consist of influential local people, such as bureaucrats, civil servants, clerics, intellectuals, and businessmen and businesswomen. Through these first meetings, the movement participants find an opportunity to articulate their motivations for starting up educational and cultural activities in this new community.

The main purpose of selecting the first contacts from those who are influential in the local area is neither political nor elitist. Rather, it is based on the understanding that such people possess an ability to mobilize their society and help certain ideas take root far faster than any other people can. In addition, through these interpersonal relations, the participants in the Gülen movement build trust with the local authorities by going to them and introducing the vision of the movement even before the local authorities learn about their existence and start investigating the movement's purpose. Moreover, movement participants continue their relationship with the local authorities, assuring them that they are willing to be continuously monitored by local officials with regard to their activities.[25]

The next chapter examines the discourse of the movement participants based on the teachings and writings of Gülen himself. In this discourse, the overarching concept is the idea of *hizmet* (serving one's fellow human beings). The chapter explores the movement's core concepts and ideas, while later chapters link these ideas with their reception among the local individuals in a particular social setting. These chapters demonstrate that it is not merely the ideas of the movement that matter, but also the mechanisms that movement activists employ on the ground in order to root their vision of society in individual communities.

3

The *Hizmet* Discourse of the Gülen Movement

> A mature person is one who would say, "After you, sir!"
> while both exiting from Hell and entering into Heaven.
>
> *M. F. Gülen*

The concepts that constitute Gülen's outlook, and thus the vision of movement activists, in this analysis, are wrapped up in the overarching concept of *hizmet* (service to one's fellow human beings). Each principle that underlies Gülen's teaching derives directly from the idea of living to serve. These principles include *gaye-i hayal* (the purpose of one's life), *diğergamlık* (altruism) and *başkası için yaşama* (living for others), *mes'uliyet duygusu* (sense of personal responsibility) and *adanmışlık ruhu* (spirit of devotion). This chapter looks at how Gülen elucidates these core concepts in his work and how they are put into practice in the conduct of the movement participants. Similarly, it tries to identify both the underlying philosophy and the operational concepts that are put into practice to analyze how the movement has spread, for looking at both structural and operational concepts provides a clearer picture of the conduct of the participants in the movement. These operational concepts include *sohbet* and *hizmet* (conversation and service), *istişare* and *mütevelli* (collective decision making and board of trustees), and *himmet* and *verme tutkusu* (personal commitment and passion for giving). Throughout the analysis, this chapter uses Gülen's original terms for these concepts, along with their English translations.

CORE CONCEPTS

Gaye-i Hayal (Purpose of One's Life)

Gülen considers *gaye-i hayal* (purpose of one's life) the key to living: one's ultimate purpose in life should be seeking the Creator's pleasure by serving the created (humanity). However, serving the created and being productive for other human beings depends on whether a person can preserve his or her well-being. What determines whether one can and does preserve one's well-being is whether one has a purpose. In his book, *Buhranlar Anaforunda İnsan* (The Human in the Whirlpool of Crisis), originally published in the 1980s, Gülen argued:

> Human generations can preserve their well-being only if they have high ideals and goals. Those who do not have goals eventually turn into walking cadavers. Every being in Nature can be fruitful, productive and benefit other beings only if it preserves its well-being. Similarly, a human can preserve his or her well-being only with high ideals, goals and his or her constant struggle and action to achieve those goals. Just like inactive materials that gradually corrode, human generations without ideals and goals, and hence inactive, are destined to be dispersed.[26]

In another work *The Statue of Our Souls*, published in English translation in 2005 (first published in 1998 as *Ruhumuzun Heykelini Dikerken*), Gülen explains the characteristics of the *mefkure insanı* (person of ideals) as follows:

A person of ideals is, first of all, a hero of love, who loves God, the Almighty Creator devotedly and feels a deep interest in the whole of creation under the wings of that love, who embraces everything and everybody with compassion, filled with an attachment to the country and people; they care for children as the buds of the future, they advise the young to become people of ideals, giving them high aims and targets; they honor the old with wholehearted regard and esteem, develop bridges over the abysses to connect and unite the different sections of society, and exert all their efforts to polish thoroughly whatever may already exist of harmony between people.[27]

Gaye-i hayal is not a concept that originates with Gülen. The concept has been scrutinized by other scholars prior to Gülen. Traditional Islamic teachings suggest that one's will and carnal self are in constant struggle with each other. While the former instructs people to do what is beneficial to the self and to fellow humans, the latter instructs the person to do whatever is pleasurable and whatever satisfies his or her desires. Hence, the latter feeds selfishness. *Gaye-i hayal* is seen as an instrument that can prevent a person's mental capabilities from being captured by his or her carnal self. In other words, *gaye-i hayal* is the concept that makes a person live for others instead of living only for himself or herself. Gülen demonstrates the practical application of *gaye-i hayal* in contemporary modern life.

Gaye-i hayal is one of the most frequently repeated themes in Gülen's writings and public speeches. He articulates his *gaye-i hayal* as achieving global peace through helping nations educate their new generations with such universal ethical values as dialogue, tolerance, altruism, and positive patriotism. Patriotism seems contradictory to the former values, given that nationalism has been the main driving force behind most of the wars and conflicts in the last three centuries.

Thomas Michel stresses that the Gülen-inspired schools aim to raise patriotic individuals who are well-versed in their own nations' histories and have national pride but are not prejudiced about other nationalities.[28] Michel argues that Gülen views national pride as the *sine qua non* for new generations to determine a clear vision for their nations. Gülen believes that his *gaye-i hayal* of achieving global peace can only be fulfilled by raising individuals who share common ethical values that are shared by all religions, races, and nationalities. According to Ali Ünal, Gülen's advising his audience to open schools is only a strategy employed to fulfill that *gaye-i hayal*.[29]

How does *gaye-i hayal* relate to the chief criticism usually leveled at Gülen that he aims to create a state based on Islamic principles? The ultra-secular factions of the state establishment[30] in Turkey have consistently speculated that Gülen's ultimate goal—and thus the basis of his teachings—is to establish an Islamic state. When the movement reached out first to countries in Central Asia and the Caucasus and then to those in Southeast Asia by the late 1990s, the same small group in the establishment accused Gülen of conspiring to establish a global Islamic state. Gülen has responded to these accusations by advising people to visit the schools and institutions that have been associated with him and see with their own eyes whether any sort of Islamic agenda is being carried out. In 1997, Gülen proposed that the Turkish state take over the schools if they were a threat to the secular regime, and he suggested that he would even encourage the local entrepreneurs, educators, and parents who had established these schools to turn them over to the state. In addition, he has consistently stressed that he has no ties to these schools other than merely encouraging people to establish similar schools as often as they can.[31] During the same year, the political Islamist Welfare

Party, which was the ruling party at the time and was later banned by the country's Constitutional Court, sought to build a mosque in the middle of Taksim Square, the most liberal and secular part of Istanbul. Gülen criticized the Welfare Party for its policy and suggested that it build a school.[32]

There is also some evidence that people in the secular camp who initially opposed Gülen have changed their views about him and the movement as they have familiarized themselves with the schools and other institutions. My own informants stressed the transformation of their own views over time. Cengiz Aydoğdu, a prominent journalist in Mardin notes, "We, the social democrats, heard about Gülen initially through the media only, and hence viewed him as a fanatical Muslim leader. However, as we have had a chance to observe the educational services that the movement has provided, and as we have participated in their cultural activities, we have realized that the Gülen movement is nothing other than an 'education campaign' and Gülen is a sincere Muslim in his own way."[33] Similarly, Ziya Ayhan, a senior member of a small business association states, "I am politically leftist and do not share Gülen's worldview. However, I find the Gülen movement volunteers quite successful in the field of education and occasionally participate in their activities. My daughter goes to the Sur university preparatory course which has been founded by Gülen movement volunteers. I trust them."[34] In a similar vein, Ahmet Yusuf, a practicing lawyer in Istanbul, stresses that "the Gülen-inspired schools all around the world have been under the strict scrutiny of about ninety countries, and none of these countries has considered these schools a threat to themselves. Therefore, what a militant secularist group in Turkey says does not make any sense."[35]

Diğergamlık and *Başkası İçin Yaşama* (Altruism and Living for Others)

Altruism or selflessness and living for others in the broadest sense, are prerequisites for a person to dedicate himself or herself to an overarching *gaye-i hayal* of serving fellow humans:

> Just like a tree can grow in direct proportion to the strength of its roots, man can improve himself and elevate spiritually in proportion to his ability to avoid selfishness and thinking of self-interest.[36]

According to Gülen, *diğergamlık* (altruism) is an essential characteristic of a person who is dedicated to a grand ideal, such as serving society. He considers *diğergamlık* a source of strength that prepares a person to face all sorts of difficulties that can be encountered when trying to live for something beyond oneself:

> Those who strive to enlighten others, seek happiness for them, and extend a helping hand, have such a developed and enlightened spirit that they are like guardian angels. They struggle with disasters befalling society, stand up to "storms," hurry to put out "fire," and are always on the alert for possible shocks.[37]

Gülen views the individual of *gaye-i hayal* as such an altruist that he or she is willing to tackle society's most burdensome problems on behalf of its other members. According to Enes Ergene, the grand ideal of living for others is the main dynamic that Gülen thinks can lead to a society's revival. Ergene argues that without the heroes and heroines who are dedicated to the grand ideal to the extent that Gülen describes, it is impossible for society even to preserve its identity and values inherited from historical experience, let alone carry out a renaissance or revival.[38]

With regard to the prerequisites of a social revival, Gülen describes the characteristics of those heroic individuals who would carry out that revival:

> Today, more than anything else, we need heroic individuals who will say, "I will be happy to step into the Hellfire for the happiness and well-being of my fellow humans," …who, putting their interests and selfishness aside, are devoted to society, …who will willingly suffer on behalf of society, …who, with the torch of science and reason in hand, illuminate people and struggle against ignorance and unkindness, …who, with a great resolve and dedication, extend help to anyone in need, …who, without losing their hope in the face of the difficulties on their way, will continue to do so, …who, forgetting their desire to live, will rejoice in the pleasure of letting live.[39]

Gülen emphasizes that just as important as having altruistic and dedicated heroic individuals is the necessity of these individuals' collective action; a collective revival is possible only through the individual revival that must precede it. In this way, Gülen views collective and individual revival as mutually dependent:

> Every plan and project for individual revival without a motivation for collective revival and vice versa is nothing but wishful thinking.[40]

For Gülen, individual life and collective-social life are strictly dependent on each other. Even if for a period of time each could occur independently, neither would be able to preserve its own existence without the other. Ergene argues that Gülen's heavy emphasis on collective action results from the Qur'anic teaching on human nature, "Humanity is not fond of charity by default; rather, humanity is inclined to obstruct it naturally."[41] In other words, not only are individuals not inclined to do charity work without an immediate incentive, but they are also inclined to prevent others from doing the charity work that they fail to do. Even if some individuals want to do charity work, it can be quite difficult for them to do so consistently unless there are others doing the same thing. However, collective action eliminates such obstructive individual tendencies that would sooner or later halt individual efforts to live altruistically. Gülen considers reviving the ideal of living for others in the minds and hearts of individuals as the ultimate responsibility.[42] He believes that once individuals adopt and keep struggling to fulfill such an ultimate responsibility, their idle energy will be activated and hence collective action will be sustained.[43]

Reading Gülen's statements selectively about the characteristics of individuals who have *gaye-i hayal* could naturally make one inclined to ask whether Gülen is seeking to create a sort of vanguard of individuals who possess all of these merits and hence would lead the rest of society. After all, it would be quite optimistic, even if Gülen does not seem to think it so, to imagine the majority of society being as dedicated as those Gülen describes in his teachings. If this is the case, is he trying to single out a select group of people who can seize control of society?

Gülen avoids specifying a certain group or socio-economic class as his target audience. Instead, he seeks to convey his message to any individual of any socio-economic status or of any ethno-religious identity. Similarly, instead of one's features present at birth, he exalts certain values and characteristics that every person can adopt and develop through individual effort regardless of ethnicity, religion, nationality or socio-economic status. The "person of heart" (*gönül insanı*), for instance, seems to be the ultimate definition that Gülen uses to describe the characteristics of people dedicated to serving their fellow humans:

> The person of heart is a monument of humility and auster-ity, who is adjusted to spiritual life, who is constantly alert against material and physical desires, and who is resolute to stay away from hatred, vanity, jealousy, and selfishness.[44]

One can observe that Gülen's universal call has been received by people of different identities, backgrounds, and socio-economic strata. Individuals who become involved with the Gülen movement adopt its vision in proportion to their adoption of Gülen's values. Therefore, the variation among individuals' involvement and responsibilities within the movement depends on how much responsibility they are willing to assume. The accessibility of Gülen's ideas to everyone involved in the movement and subjection of these ideas to individual interpretations ensure checks and balances within the movement and, hence, the absence of a certain vanguard that interprets and applies rules.

Mes'uliyet Duygusu
(Sense of Personal Responsibility)

The sense of personal responsibility (*mes'uliyet duygusu*) is a crucial concept in both adopting and practicing the *hizmet* discourse. The concept is derived from the Islamic belief that every individual will be held accountable for the way he or she has lived and has spent the time and energy bestowed upon him or her in this world. The Qur'an offers the belief that simply states that every individual will be resurrected in the afterlife and held accountable for every moment that he or she spent in this world.[45] The Qur'an urges believers to use their lives wisely and invest in the afterlife. In a similar fashion, Prophet Muhammad says, "The world is the field of the afterlife," that is, whatever one sows in this life will be harvested in the afterlife.

Subscribing to this school of thought, Gülen notes:

> For me, the worldly life is only a small part of the life that has started in the realm of souls and will continue indefinitely either in Heaven or in Hell in the afterlife. And since one's afterlife is shaped by it, the worldly life is of the utmost importance. Therefore, the worldly life should be used in order to earn the afterlife and to please the One who has bestowed it. The way to do so is to seek to please God and, as an inseparable dimension of it, to serve immediate family members, society, country, and all of humanity accordingly. This service is our right, and sharing it with others is our duty.[46]

If there is one concept that explains the individual mobility that has brought the Gülen movement into being, it is *mes'uliyet duygusu*, the sense of personal responsibility, regardless of whether others fulfill their responsibilities or not. In other words, individually mobilized by the *mes'uliyet duygusu*, people come together and constitute a collectively mobilized group.

While explaining the difference between *cemaat* (community) and *cemiyet* (social organization), Gülen says that the community associated with his ideas is a natural outcome of the gathering of those individuals who have independently felt responsible for serving others. That is, while *cemiyet* is a result of individuals who have organized or been brought together in a hierarchical structure in order to achieve certain common objectives, the movement inspired by Gülen's ideas is, in contrast, a result of the gathering of those who have felt personally responsible for fulfilling a similar objective.

Gülen suggests that the community gathered for a certain prayer is basically a natural outcome of the gathering of ordinary (and not necessarily related) individuals who have felt the need to be there and perform that prayer at that time. By the same token, he explains, ordinary, unrelated individuals have come together to establish schools and carry out cultural activities due to their belief in the necessity of education, dialogue, and tolerance.[47] What Gülen has provided, then, is a road map for transforming collective energy into productive endeavors directed toward all of humanity. As we will see in detail in the following chapters, the most notable end result of such a transformation has been the proliferation of schools, university preparatory courses, and reading halls established by individuals who share Gülen's ideas.

Adanmışlık Ruhu and *Gönül İnsanı* (The Spirit of Devotion and the Person of Heart)

According to Gülen, *adanmışlık ruhu* (the spirit of devotion) is the state of living in complete dedication to the service of humanity and seeking to please God in so doing. In relation to *adanmışlık ruhu*, Gülen introduces another concept, *gönül insanı* (the person of heart), to describe a person who is dedicated to serving humanity and the Creator. *Gönül insanı* is simply one who possesses *adanmışlık ruhu* and hence lives a life fully dedicated to serving humanity and God. He stresses that nothing other than this could be such a person's goal:

> The most significant features and the most reliable strength of those who have dedicated themselves to the ideal of spending their lives in the quest to please God and be loved by Him are that they have neither material nor spiritual expectations. In the reckonings and plans of those dedicated to seeking God's pleasure, the concepts of cost, benefit, labor, revenue, wealth, and comfort on which many worldly people put great emphasis have absolutely no significance. These concepts never constitute a criterion.[48]

Moreover, he describes the implications of *adanmışlık ruhu* (the spirit of devotion) for one's daily activities:

> The philosophy of devotion instructs the individual to live in adherence to high ideals, self-sacrifice from the simplest pleasures such as eating and drinking, preferring a rather simple life for the well-being and comfort of society.[49]

It is easy to observe the same philosophy of devotion ruling the lives of ordinary individuals ranging from teachers working in the Gülen-inspired schools to local people sponsoring the schools and all other cultural activities. Thomas Michel, the Vatican representative for interfaith dialogue, illustrates the extent of this devotion by reporting on a blacksmith he met during his visit to southeastern Turkey who said, "I have a school that I am sponsoring in South Africa, and that's why I am working."[50] Similarly, Vahit Atak, a Mardinian businessman who sponsored the construction of Atak High School in Mardin, notes, "The well-educated teachers whom we saw in the university preparatory courses opened by the volunteers of the Gülen movement could normally earn a salary at least three times greater than they earned in Mardin. Yet, they preferred to come to Mardin, where nobody would come unless they had to."[51] Such self-sacrifice is likely to be seen at every level within the movement, regardless of one's socio-economic status or gender. To a greater or lesser extent, every individual affiliated with the movement has the ideal of achieving the spiritual status of *gönül insanı* (the person of heart).

Being a *gönül insanı* (person of heart) means simply that the person is involved in a constant struggle with his or her carnal self and material and spiritual pleasures; it is to have no motivation other than pleasing God through serving His subjects, all humanity:

> A person of heart constantly struggles with himself or herself. Since such people are always busy seeking their faults and fallacies, they do not seek to find others' faults and fallacies. They tolerate others' faults. They respond with a smile to the misbehavior of others and with good deeds to mistreatment, and never consider breaking the heart of anyone, even if their own hearts have been broken fifty times.[52] Similarly, people of heart carry out their every action and activity in the belief that this world is the realm of service but not of reward. They view serving humanity as the most crucial duty on the way to pleasing the Creator. And no matter how big and important are the accomplishments that they achieve, they never think of attributing the success to themselves and never seek a reward for that accomplishment.[53]

So, *gönül insanı* (person of heart), just like *gaye-i hayal* (purpose of one's life), *diğergamlık* (altruism), *başkası için yaşama* (living for others), *mes'uliyet duygusu* (sense of personal responsibility), and *adanmışlık ruhu* (spirit of devotion), can be viewed as a key concept that elucidates certain patterns of behavior one can observe within the Gülen movement. It is difficult to explain in any way the local people's resolve to sponsor the movement's educational activities other than to say that they view the values that Gülen has put forth as the core values of their faith and seek to deepen their faith by practicing those values in their daily lives. One can simply conclude that these are the core concepts that explain the motivations of individuals who somehow participate in and promote the activities of the movement.

STRUCTURAL AND OPERATIONAL CONCEPTS

Beside the core concepts that elucidate the behavioral patterns of those inspired by Fethullah Gülen, there are certain concepts that underlie the structure and operations of the movement. These concepts include *hizmet* (service), *sohbet* (conversation gathering), *istişare* (collective decision making), *mütevelli* (board of trustees), *himmet* (personal commitment), and *verme tutkusu* (passion for giving).

Sohbet and *Hizmet* (Conversation and Service)

If *hizmet* is the sum of values and practices that instruct one to serve one's community, *sohbet* is the medium through which the necessity for *hizmet* is communicated to individuals. *Sohbet* has various meanings, such as "pleasant conversation, verbal exchange on a certain subject within a group of individuals, and engaging in fellowship."[54] Operationally, however, within the practices of the Gülen movement, the meaning of *sohbet* goes beyond mere conversation and becomes a routine activity utilized by the movement participants to cultivate a sense of service, reach out to ever more individuals, and share the educational vision with new people. *Sohbet* is a platform where individuals find an opportunity to socialize, chat, and exchange ideas about their projects (either education- or business-related), but absolutely nothing about politics or such potentially divisive subjects as nationalism, ethnicity, and regionalism. These are generally avoided in the *sohbet,* since participants' differences of opinion concerning secondary issues might eventually impede their cooperation on the primary issue: building educational facilities and carrying out cultural activities to promote dialogue and tolerance among different segments of society. Therefore, the movement volunteers seek to use the *sohbet* forum to cultivate a sense of commonality, address common needs and goals as opposed to differences, and communicate the necessity of *hizmet* (literally "service," used to mean "altruistic service for the good of others").

The *sohbet* groups are mostly organized according to the participants' occupation, as long as there is a sufficient number of people, which could be as low as three or four participants. For instance, public servants group together with their fellows, while businessmen do so with other business owners. The main idea of grouping the same or similar job holders, which is not ultimately necessary, is again to increase the commonalities among the *sohbet* meetings' participants so that they can better socialize, share their experiences, and network with each other. For the businessmen, these meetings also provide an opportunity to get to know potential business partners, customers or suppliers.

Efforts of volunteers in the Gülen movement to awaken a sense of *hizmet* at the public level have had broad implications for the community in Mardin, the main focus of my empirical research. *Sohbet* meetings with those involved in the health-care sector emphasize such values as self-sacrifice, altruism, and living for others rather more when compared to those meetings involving workers or businessmen. *Sohbet* participants in the health-care services seek to encourage each other to stay in Mardin or at least in southeastern Turkey, instead of leaving for either their hometowns or for the bigger cities in western Turkey. They consider their service as doctors or clinicians in Mardin as a way to express their devotion and self-sacrifice to the Creator through serving their fellow humans.

Participants study passages from various sources, but mostly from Gülen's works, since his teachings directly promote the values of the *hizmet* discourse. The reading activity is not necessarily led by one person. Most of the time, participants take turns reading and leading the discussion during the meeting. The participants I have met reported that these weekly meetings keep them motivated to serve in a region where resources are quite limited, the patient–doctor ratio extremely high, and social life almost non-existent.[55]

The *sohbet* meetings among local businessmen and workers are carried out in a way similar to those carried out among health-care specialists, for the same values of self-sacrifice, altruism, and living for others are emphasized. However, in contrast to the health-care *sohbet* meetings, which aim to keep those service workers dedicated to serving in southeastern Turkey, those of the businessmen are intended to encourage participants to devote themselves to developing educational facilities in Mardin. The main reason for this is that workers and businessmen are mostly local Mardinians, as opposed to the health-care specialists, who are mostly from the more developed western cities.[56]

The *sohbet* meetings also serve as a seminar to help moderate the views of some local mosque imams, who sometimes sympathize with radical Islamist groups. One local businessman, who volunteers to organize such meetings with the imams, stresses the moderating effects of the *sohbet* meetings on those imams who are fond of such groups as Hizbullah[57] and al-Qaeda. He notes, "In the beginning, some of the imams despised us as 'light' Muslims. They criticized us for not taking up arms and embarking on an armed struggle or establishing a political party to pursue an Islamic regime. Gülen's teachings about Islam seemed sort of heretical to them. However, as we kept reading and discussing the values of Islam as Gülen has interpreted them clearly in his writings, those imams gradually moderated their opinions and realized that violence is not the way of Islam. Now they are asking why we did not start those sohbet meetings earlier."[58] The meetings' moderating effect on the radical-leaning imams, promises minimization, if not eradication, of Islamist fundamentalism in Mardin, where it is believed that there are still forty to fifty unofficial religious schools.[59]

İstişare and Mütevelli (Collective Decision Making and Board of Trustees)

The *sohbet* meetings where the *hizmet* discourse is communicated to the local people provide a pool of individuals who volunteer to come together in *istişare* (collective decision making) meetings to ponder how to carry out the education projects. Gülen reportedly consults and is consulted by his immediate friends and the community in general on issues ranging from his daily life to the activities and projects of the movement participants. Also, he urges everyone to do the same both in their daily lives and in everything regarding the projects of the movement. Gülen advises:

> The important things which should be noted are: consultation is the first condition for the success of a decision

made on any issue. We have all seen how all decisions made without having been thought through thoroughly, without having taken into account the views and criticisms of others, whether related to individuals in particular or to society in general, have resulted in fiasco, loss, and great disappointment. Even if a person has a superior nature and outstanding intellect, if they are content with their own opinions and are not receptive and respectful to the opinions of others, then they are more prone to make mistakes and errors than the average person. The most intelligent person is the one who most appreciates and respects mutual consultation and deliberation (*mashwarat*), and who benefits most from the ideas of others.[60]

Gülen's sensitivity to consulting with his friends is emulated by the individuals who are, to varying degrees, involved with the movement. The more involved they are with the activities of the movement, the more they seem to strive to apply the principle of *istişare* in their conduct. As we will see in detail in the following chapter, in Mardin the teachers in the university preparatory courses and the local Mardin people who have sponsored the various educational projects have repeatedly held *istişare*s before opening each university preparatory course and private school, as well as organizing public events where they share their vision with the rest of the Mardin community. Given the role of *istişare* within the Gülen movement and the emphasis on collective decision making, the movement seems to function horizontally rather than vertically.

Operationally, the concept of *mütevelli*, or essentially a board of trustees, has meant that the movement relies on several small groups of individuals who have volunteered to take on relatively more responsibility, whether overseeing more projects or donating more money when compared to other individuals. The *mütevelli* circle is open to anyone who consistently carries out the responsibilities that fall on his or her shoulders.

Himmet and *Verme Tutkusu* (Personal Commitment and Passion for Giving)

Personal commitment (*himmet*) is another key concept that relates to both *istişare* and *mütevelli*. In essence, it refers to one's personal commitment to carrying out the duty at hand, be it sponsoring a school project or reaching out to as many people as possible to share the movement's educational vision. Operationally, *himmet* seems to be a *sine qua non* for one's contribution to fulfilling the educational vision. In other words, the more one commits—be it money, time or effort—the more one cares about the success of the education projects. The act of giving or committing itself seems to be more important than the amount given or the sort of commitment. *Himmet* is, in this way, a sort of instrument to tame one's carnal self through sacrifice. However, *himmet* does not seem to be a prerequisite for involvement in the activities of the Gülen movement.

"Those who sense the pleasure of giving become sort of crazy for giving,"[61] remarks Asılsoy, a local Mardin businessman who donates a sizeable proportion of his annual income to the ongoing education projects carried out in Mardin. He recalls that he promised himself that he would donate ten times more the following year than the amount he had donated the first time he had participated in a *himmet* meeting (at a fundraising dinner), which had been for the construction of the first university preparatory course in Mardin. For Davut Bey, another local Mardinian who has been active in carrying out educational projects from the very beginning, *himmet* (personal commitment) does not mean only "donating whatever you have on your own, but it also means promising to procure."[62] In this regard, he recalls his and his friends' frequent trips to such large cities as Istanbul, Ankara, and Izmir to solicit support from wealthy businessmen who are originally from Mardin in the form of both cash and supplies. For those who have willingly assumed the responsibility to donate and procure resources, *himmet* seems to have turned into a passion for giving (*verme tutkusu*). Among these people who are "crazy for giving," as Asılsoy puts it, the common denominator of both a peddler and a prominent business leader is the passion for giving. What varies is only the amount of their donations or the extent of their commitment.

In conclusion, having a *gaye-i hayal* is one of the most emphasized subjects in Gülen's writings and public speeches. He considers it to be crucial to one's life and suggests that one's ultimate goal should be seeking the Creator's pleasure by serving humanity. Gülen finds a direct relation between one's having a *gaye-i hayal* and one's well-being. That is, one can live a productive life only if one has an ultimate ideal that serves the common good of society or all of humanity. An individual who lacks such an ideal, glorifies his or her own interests, and judges himself or herself according to the standards of society essentially becomes a walking cadaver who will, sooner or later, lose his or her spiritual essence, even if he or she remains physically alive. With regard to this, Gülen attributes the utmost importance to having a *gaye-i hayal* for one's spiritual development.

Gülen introduces two complementary concepts that enable one to live one's life dedicated to an overarching *gaye-i hayal* (purpose of one's life): *diğergamlık* (altruism) and *başkası için yaşama* (living for others). He considers altruism and living only in order to be of benefit to fellow human beings as the essential source of strength for a person with *gaye-i hayal*. Gülen never specifies a certain group of people based upon their socio-economic status, ethnicity, religion or nationality; rather, he promotes universally accepted ethical values that anyone can adopt.

Furthermore, he introduces the concepts of *mes'uliyet duygusu* (sense of personal responsibility), and *adanmışlık ruhu* (spirit of devotion) as two mobilizing factors that enable one to adopt the notion of serving one's fellow human beings as a grand purpose. Although *gaye-i hayal* and *diğergamlık* (altruism)/*başkası için yaşama* (living for other) complement each other and enable one to dedicate oneself to serving humanity, *mes'uliyet duygusu* (sense of personal responsibility) is the notion that encourages the individual to adopt the former two concepts and practice them in daily life. *Adanmışlık ruhu* (spirit of devotion) is another complementary characteristic that instructs one to remain motivated and focus one's attention on pleasing the Creator through serving His subjects.

4

Emergence and Development
in Mardin

Historical Background

The development of the Gülen movement in Mardin has taken place in such a way that it can be explained, to a great extent, by using the diffusion theory developed by McAdam and Rucht to explain the spread of social movements. However, it also presents a unique example of a particular social movement mobilizing individuals who were not previously engaged in any form of collective action, in a non-familiar community. In that sense, as opposed to the diffusion theory model of social movement–social movement interaction, the Gülen movement presents a model of social movement–individual actors. In other words, the diffusion theory model requires the existence of a social movement in the new community that can cooperate with the social movement that intends to diffuse into that community. The Gülen movement, however, does not cooperate with another social movement that is already active in the community. Instead, volunteers make contact with local individuals, share their vision with them, and mobilize with them to realize that vision in that particular community.[63]

McAdam and Rucht have drawn attention to the role of inter- and intra-movement relations in understanding the spread of social movements. According to their model of the cross-national diffusion of ideas, the initial interpersonal relations encourage the identification of activist-adopters in one country with the activist-transmitters in another. Once the first contact has been made, the inter-movement relations are strengthened through such non-relational channels as media and literature. According to this model, the diffusion of one social movement into another country consists of four fundamental components: the transmitter or emitter (person, group or organization), the adopter (person, group or organization), the item that is diffused (material goods, information or skills), and a channel of diffusion that links the transmitter and the adopter (media, press or persons).

The way the Gülen movement has spread into Mardin satisfies McAdam and Rucht's model in that the spreading process has involved all four of the model's components: Gülen movement activists are the transmitters; Mardinian local people (individuals) are the adopters; Gülen's educational vision is the item that has been conveyed; and, lastly, such activities as fellowship circles, books, audio cassettes, and trips are channels of diffusion. However, its spread into Mardin also exhibits a unique characteristic that is not described in McAdam and Rucht's model. Their model requires the presence of transmitting and adopting social movements as equivalent counterparts. That is, their model portrays the diffusion of social movements as sharing ideas and practices and strengthening relations between two social movements in different societies. Even if the forms of transmitter and adopter vary (e.g., person–person, person–organization or organization–organization), eventually the social movement that is to be diffused carries out that diffusion in cooperation with another active social movement that exists in the new setting. However, the Gülen movement spreads through the mobilization of individuals in the new setting, including those who are not necessarily attached to each other. Its diffusion consists of the four fundamental components found in the model of the cross-national diffusion of a movement's ideas; however, the adopter is not a "social movement" but "individuals." In this regard, the case of the diffusion of the Gülen movement into Mardin contributes to understanding how social movements spread through mobilizing individuals.

The diffusion of the movement into Mardin started in 1988 with one young man's visit with Fatih Asılsoy, a hardware store owner who would soon be the first and foremost Mardinian to foster the Gülen movement's educational activities. Asılsoy notes that he began to learn about the Gülen movement and its educational vision through his frequent "tea conversations" with a young man who was doing his military service in Mardin at the time.[64] It took almost a year for this person to tell Asılsoy about Gülen, who was a prominent Turkish Islamic scholar and viewed as a leader of a contemporary faith-based civil society movement. Asılsoy attributes the young man's reluctance at that first meeting to the ongoing political conditions in Turkey and to the existing peculiarities of Mardin at that time.

In general, faith-based or Muslim social movements have been welcomed by the public, especially by people who practice the interpretation of Islam, while radical movements have not found popular support. Nevertheless, the ultra-secular state establishment in Turkey has always viewed all sorts of Islamic movements as a threat to the secular regime and, therefore, has suppressed their development severely. Due to such official policies, several unsuccessful attempts have been made to prosecute Gülen himself for allegedly "establishing a religious enterprise against the secular regime."[65] While such Islamic movements as the Nakshibandi and Kadiri Sufi orders, as well as such moderate Islamic communities as the Nur movement,[66] have been quite popular in Turkish society, the ongoing Hizbullah[67] experience in the southeastern region (which includes Mardin) in the late 1980s and early 1990s made the local people "extremely suspicious of any social movement that has a religious characteristic,"[68] as Imam Abdulbari of Nusaybin notes. Hizbullah's frequent civilian killings in the region, which it justified on the basis of Wahhabi principles, have made "the local people quite cautious about religious movements,"[69] stresses Murat Salim, a local store owner in Nusaybin. In addition to all of these likely reasons, the "emergency status" in the entire southeastern region due to the PKK problem (the separatist Kurdish terrorist organization) brought many civil initiatives under official scrutiny in Mardin.

Under these circumstances, Fatih Asılsoy and the young man developed a strong friendship through weekly tea conversations (*sohbets*),[70] during which they pondered the chronic problems of Mardin, such as the lack of sufficient education facilities, the increasing number of unskilled and unemployed youth, and the concomitant problem of unemployed youth joining either the PKK or Hizbullah. These *sohbet*s, which started with only Asılsoy and the young man in 1988, continued and attracted more people from Asılsoy's immediate friendship circle and other Mardin businessmen and workers through 1991.

THE FIRST *SOHBET* GROUP

Between 1988 and 1991, periodic *sohbet* meetings served as an agent of outreach. These meetings took place in the participants' houses on a rotating basis, and through them more people were brought to understand the necessity of doing something to combat the deprivations in the city, especially in the field of education. Most of them agreed that the state was unable to provide the necessary education services not only in Mardin but in all of southeastern Turkey. In fact, some of them even thought that the ultra-secular state deliberately deprived the region of schools and other basic services to punish the region's Kurdish population. Either way, the unchanging realities were that the number of unemployed and uneducated youth in Mardin was steadily increasing and that these people constituted the main recruitment source for both PKK and Hizbullah.[71] Eventually, they all agreed that the local people would have to bear the responsibility of tackling the education problem in Mardin.

Once the "consciousness for education" campaign reached a certain point within the *sohbet* group, the individuals who were more aware of the education service projects of Gülen movement volunteers and the corresponding vision of education brought up the idea of actually establishing such institutions. Starting with the Yamanlar and Fatih high schools in Izmir and in Istanbul, respectively, in 1982,[72] the success of Gülen-inspired institutions in the field of education had gained the public's approval. As a result, the process of establishing the schools has continued in different Turkish cities ever since.

Amid the increasing deficiency of state-funded public schools, these Gülen-inspired schools seem to have distinguished themselves from their counterparts by their well-rounded and research-based education and their unprecedented success in international science contests.[73] For the first time, Turkey was winning championships in science contests because of the efforts of students attending the Fatih and Yamanlar high schools. More importantly, these schools were established and run as a result of completely civic initiatives. In that sense, they constituted a model for people in other cities. The success of the schools has sent out the resounding message that the citizens themselves can solve their education problems and cannot expect everything from the state. In fact, the Fatih and Yamanlar examples meant that the public could handle the education issue much better than the state.[74]

After becoming acquainted with Gülen's educational paradigm, people in different cities began to visit these two high schools to see how this vision was applied. They then embarked on building similar schools in their own cities. These businessmen were mostly those who had been attending Gülen's public sermons, in which he frequently emphasized the importance of education and called for the building of modern schools instead of mosques. Basically, he used his growing public popularity to encourage people to increase the number of such schools. In other words, one successful school in one city triggered the construction of similar schools in different cities. Hasan Doğru, a businessman who funded the entire construction of a school in the city of Kilis in 1997, noted that he decided to do so after his visits to the Fatih, Yamanlar, and Samanyolu high schools in Istanbul, Izmir, and Ankara, respectively.[75] Another school whose construction was triggered in this way is Sunguroğlu High School in Gaziantep, a relatively more developed city adjacent to Mardin.

Throughout this period, Gülen-inspired schools proliferated in different cities and gained one success after another in both the national university admissions tests and in international science contests. The local people of Mardin learned about these schools through the media. Eventually, the *sohbet*s that had started in Mardin in 1988 were coupled with frequent trips to Gaziantep in order to see what the educational vision of the Gülen movement was actually about.

A LEARNING EXPERIENCE

During these trips, the still small Mardin *sohbet* group found an opportunity to see Sunguroğlu High School and the university preparatory courses in Gaziantep and to meet with teachers and businessmen who, respectively, taught at and funded these institutions. For about three years, until late 1991, one trip to Gaziantep followed another, as Asılsoy put it. Through these trips, the Mardin businessmen in the *sohbet* group both strengthened their relations with each other and their belief in the common cause of Mardin's education campaign, which had been the main topic of their meetings. More importantly, actually seeing the practical application of the movement's educational vision caused them to realize that the whole education campaign was not mere rhetoric, but had practical applications.

As the Mardin businessmen visited Sunguroğlu High School, they imagined the same school established in Mardin, a city that faced the chronic problems of insufficient numbers of both schools and teachers. In addition, when they saw students at the university preparatory course in Gaziantep, they imagined the unemployed youth of their city attending these courses and becoming eligible to attend university and thereby avoiding falling prey to either PKK or Hizbullah recruitment.[76] As well as the students and the facilities, the teachers and businessmen affiliated with these schools deeply impressed the Mardin *sohbet* group. In many ways, these trips to Gaziantep were a learning experience for the Mardin group.

The group had a chance to observe certain values of *hizmet* discourse[77] in the daily lives of the Gaziantep teachers and businessmen associated with the city's Gülen-inspired schools. Hayri Bey of Mardin notes, "Most of us were quite impressed to see teachers, who were originally ethnic Turks from modern western cities like Istanbul and Izmir, coming to the underdeveloped Southeast and preparing ethnic Kurdish or Arab students for the university admissions test."[78] He stresses that these teachers, with their degrees from Turkey's top universities, could easily have got high-paying jobs in one of the western cities; however, they had decided to come to southeastern Turkey, a place to which teachers usually come only if they have to. Similarly, Davut Bey notes, "We were stunned to see the teachers' dedication. After teaching classes for eight hours a day, they would stay until eleven o'clock at night or midnight in order to assist the students with their studies in the dormitories. They would do so without extra payment."[79] More pragmatically, Fatih Asılsoy notes, "Teachers were quite dedicated, but I did not think that they were likely to come and teach in Mardin just as they do in Gaziantep. After all, Mardin was much more deprived socio-economically and insecure, due to the PKK and Hizbullah problems, compared to Gaziantep."[80]

The Gaziantep businessmen's dedication and self-sacrifice matched that of the teachers. Hayri Bey stresses that he had never witnessed people competing with each other to donate more for a school building project until he attended a *himmet* (personal commitment) meeting in Gaziantep during one of these trips. Erhan Bey emphasizes that the people who donated in these meetings included not only businessmen, but also workers, teachers, and civil servants, and that their common characteristic was "the passion for giving."[81] He stresses that regardless of the size of their income, these people were eager to donate a sizeable amount of their annual income or monthly salaries for the construction of schools and dormitories. Asılsoy offers the concept of *ihlas* (purity of intention), another theme that Gülen has frequently stressed, to explain this extraordinary behavior. *Ihlas* means to seek only God's pleasure in one's work.

These people, including both the teachers and the sponsors, believed that they could achieve real *ihlas* through self-sacrifice with no expectation of any sort.[82] What the Mardin *sohbet* group saw in these people's behavior and daily interaction was actually nothing other than the values of *hizmet* discourse that Gülen has cultivated and communicated through his public meetings and writings since the early 1960s. Observing the discourse values on site, the Mardin *sohbet* group has, in this way, transferred know-how from Gaziantep to Mardin in order to mirror the education activities in its own city.

THE FIRST *İSTİŞARE* MEETING

The educational vision of the Gülen movement started to materialize in Mardin in late 1991. After its prolonged involvement with the Gaziantep *sohbet* group, explains Asılsoy, the Mardin *sohbet* group succeeded in bringing Akif Bey, an experienced teacher in Gaziantep's Sunguroğlu High School, to Mardin in order to coordinate the city's prospective education projects. Simultaneously, the Mardin group internalized the *hizmet* discourse, as it was the first time the Mardin group had gathered to determine an agenda in the *istişare*, which took place two days after Akif Bey arrived. The main item on the agenda, notes Asılsoy, was to locate a building to house the first college preparatory course in Mardin that the Gülen movement volunteers planned to provide.[83]

After a long search, the group found a city-government-owned, four-storey, half-ruined building in Upper Mardin.[84] Akif Bey and Asılsoy contacted the city council and the governor in order to rent the building. Asılsoy reports, "Neither the council members nor the governor believed that we could accomplish the university preparatory course project."[85] The council was reluctant to rent the building, arguing that just like previous educational projects, the group would collect tuition fees from local people, register their children, and then run away after a few months because of the city's socio-economic and security conditions. In response, Asılsoy reassured the council by offering his business and other possessions as collateral against this occurring. During the bargaining process, one council member clandestinely asked for a bribe and guaranteed that he could persuade the council to rent the building at a cheaper price and for a longer period. However, Akif Bey strictly opposed this proposal, saying that "we cannot serve our legal cause by illegal means!"[86] Asılsoy stresses that Akif Bey's reaction to that bribery proposal, a routine part of daily interaction in Mardin, and his sensitivity to any sort of illegality taught the Mardin group a lesson: the *hizmet* discourse and illegality are mutually exclusive, and those providing *hizmet* have to follow the legal path, even if doing so increases their burden. Eventually, the Mardin group rented the building for ten years.

SPONSORS AND TEACHERS WORK AS LABORERS

Using Gülen's teachings and *hizmet* discourse, Akif Bey, who also coordinated the education facilities, consistently assisted the Mardin group in adopting the *hizmet* principles. It seems that the foremost of these principles was fulfilling the *istişare* agenda: either establishing a university preparatory course or building a dormitory with their own resources, and seeking other individuals who would be willing to take responsibility for the education projects. So, Akif Bey and the other six teachers who came to teach at the yet-to-be-established university preparatory course cleaned and rebuilt the half-ruined building and encouraged the group's members to do the same. Davut Bey notes, "It was quite difficult for us to do that in the first place. After all, we all had a certain status within the Mardin community."[87]

Since he shared these feelings with Davut Bey, Asılsoy pledged to donate funds to hire workers for the reconstruction and cleaning effort. In response, Akif Bey took the money Asılsoy offered, saved it for future expenses, and continued to clean the building. On many similar occasions, Akif Bey sought to teach the Mardin group members to use their extremely limited resources wisely and not to rely on others for what they could do themselves. As the number and size of the projects grew, they hired regular workers; however, they have always adhered to the principle, 'Do as much as you can yourself and save for future projects.' Asılsoy remarks, "Working in construction and carrying out ordinary work by ourselves, which we would normally not do, we not only saved money for our future projects, but also tamed our carnal selves and developed a sense of ownership of the education projects that we would accomplish."[88]

Although this "do-it-yourself" principle of the Mardin sohbet group sometimes led to wrong interpretations, it also helped them build trust with the local authorities. On the one hand, seeing Akif Bey and the other locally well-known people unloading construction materials and remodeling the old building all by themselves, the local people in the neighborhood were quick to speculate, "Akif Bey and his friends are members of a clandestine organization and do not want to risk anyone else finding out their plans, so they did not hire any construction workers."[89] Similarly, seeing Zeynel Bey, the manager of a local bank, working in construction, one of his employees at the bank lamented, "Why didn't you tell us that you needed extra money? We could have helped you. You didn't have to work in construction."[90] Nevertheless, the group members kept working at the construction site on evenings and weekends. Doing so taught them self-sacrifice for the benefit of others, stresses Asılsoy.

On the other hand, seeing Akif Bey and other locally well-known people in the group working on a weekend, the governor of Mardin was surprised and concluded that these people were dedicated enough to accomplish the school-dormitory project they had in mind. The governor's trust in the Mardin group influenced the council's and other local bureaucrats' opinions of this group or, in other words, of the Gülen movement that soon would be personified by the Mardin group and its education projects. The group has effectively utilized the local authorities' trust in them as a reference and has sought to establish dialogue with all parts of Mardin society. Being non-political has made it easier for Gülen movement participants to develop relations with both right-wing and left-wing people in Mardin. Cihan Sancar, the mayor of Kızıltepe, stresses that she does not share Gülen's worldview, and yet she appreciates the schools and other facilities established with his vision.[91] As Orhan Tutkun, a senior administrator in the Gülen-inspired schools in Mardin, puts it, "We have friendly relations with the majority of Mardin society. More accurately, we do not have unfriendly relations with any segment of the society."[92]

THE FIRST *HIMMET* MEETING

The principle of relying on their own funds and seeking individuals who are willing to take responsibility for the education projects has been one of the most powerful mobilizing factors in the growth of the movement in Mardin and elsewhere. Relying completely on individual donations and not accepting any sort of government aid made it necessary for the movement to reach out to more people who would assume the necessary responsibility, in order to complete any project at any given time.[93] Basically, the movement had to expand in order to survive. Two concepts of *hizmet* discourse were emphasized in this growth process: *sohbet* groups and *himmet* meetings, which have complemented each other. In addition, the need for the latter necessitated the proliferation of the former, since these meetings are the arena in which people could familiarize themselves with the projects to which they would eventually commit themselves. So, the groups' proliferation depended on reaching out and sharing the educational vision with more people and getting them involved in the projects.

The Mardin *sohbet* group has overcome financial bottlenecks, as well as consequent disruptions in establishing the first university preparatory course and several other Gülen-inspired institutions in their town, by simply resorting to the *himmet* meetings. Asılsoy recalls, "When we started to rebuild

the half-ruined building, our entire fund was roughly equivalent to one thousand US dollars, which was the sum of donations from the teachers. We spent that entire fund even before
the construction was halfway done."[94] Once the funds ran out,
Akif Bey suggested holding a *himmet* meeting with the teachers and the four or five people in the *sohbet* group to procure
funds that would enable them to establish the university
preparatory course. Until then, "giving" was a merit that the
Mardin group members had heard Gülen promote frequently in his public speeches and writings and had talked about
and appreciated in their gatherings but had not practiced. The
himmet meeting included both donating and a variety of other options: seeking willing donors in either Mardin or other
cities, procuring construction materials and equipment as donations from their suppliers, committing an amount of personal physical work in the construction effort, and other things.
In fact, Akif Bey had already asked the group members to
pledge their own physical work toward cleaning the building.
Everyone in the group promised to work either after hours or
during the weekend until the construction was finished.
Therefore, they were familiar with *himmet* even if they had
not pledged their money yet.

Eventually, group members held the first *himmet* meeting. Some pledged money, some promised to seek individuals and collect the amount of money they had pledged, and
others promised to do both. The earlier trips to Gaziantep, during which the group members had had a chance to observe
himmet meetings there, made it easier to hold a similar meeting in Mardin. The donors in Gaziantep had set an example
for their counterparts in Mardin. In addition to that, the enthusiasm of the six teachers (including Akif Bey) to donate from
their limited salaries encouraged the other people in the Mardin

group to donate. That *himmet* meeting, followed by others, helped complete the establishment of the university preparatory course.

At this point, it is crucial to distinguish between a *himmet* meeting and a fund-raising meeting. In general terms, a *himmet* meeting can be viewed as a fund-raising activity, although it goes beyond mere fund raising both in style and purpose. While a fund-raising meeting emphasizes the sum of the donations collected, a *himmet* meeting emphasizes the act of "giving," regardless of the amount given.

Participants are encouraged to give (donate) as much as they can; they are encouraged to join the group of givers. In the *hizmet* discourse, the act of "giving"—meaning self-sacrifice for the good of others—is portrayed almost as worshipping God. Gülen frequently recalls the *himmet* meetings during the time of Prophet Muhammad and praises the Companions for their passion for "giving." Gülen frequently refers to the first two caliphs, Abu Bakr (who donated everything he owned) and Omar (who donated half of everything he owned), while speaking about *himmet* meetings and the act of "giving."[95] In this regard, it is not unusual to see peddlers donate half of their daily income or business owners donating half or more of their annual income. The two contemporary examples of such donors that Gülen frequently mentions are, respectively, *Lahmacuncu* Fethi ("Fethi, the sandwich-peddler*)* and Kemal Erimez, "the owner of mountains."[96] The former used to donate all of his daily revenue from selling sandwiches to the fund established for Yamanlar High School, the movement's first private school, which was established in Izmir in 1982. The latter was a rich businessman who owned diamond jewelry stores and donated his entire wealth to the funds established to open schools in Central Asia.[97] In addition to his financial donations, Kemal Erimez was actively involved in education projects and took a role in opening schools in Kazakhstan, Turkmenistan, Kyrgyzstan, and Uzbekistan, despite his advanced age. He remained in Tajikistan during the civil war in order to open the Tajik–Turk High School in Dushanbe, although the Turkish Ministry of Foreign Affairs had urged all Turkish citizens to leave because of security conditions. So, these are examples of people going beyond donating their money by becoming actively involved in the education projects of the movement and seeking to achieve God's pleasure by forcing themselves to give everything they can.

Mehmet Ali Şengül, another teacher and preacher and one of the first individuals to take part in the service projects in Turkey, notes that at a *himmet* meeting in a city in central Turkey that was attended by university students and where he was the guest speaker, "some donated money, and some who did not have money donated their watches and jackets."[98] With regards to giving, Gülen suggests that "every child must be educated to get used to 'giving,' starting at a very early age. Children should be taught that giving has more merit than taking."[99] The contemporary examples of those passionate for "giving" are businessmen and most of the teachers at the Gülen-inspired schools, who fund at least one student's monthly expenses out of their limited salaries.[100] Hadji Burhan of Midyat-Mardin notes, "The Erdem brothers, owners of Erdem Holding, were two Mardinian businessmen in Istanbul who funded the construction of the dormitory in Midyat after we visited them with a group of people from Midyat."[101] For them, *himmet* is not ordinary fund-raising but a way of worshipping God, examples of which they have seen in Prophet Muhammad's life.

In a similar fashion, along with others in the Mardin *sohbet* group, Fatih Asılsoy donated as much as he could in the first *himmet* meeting and promised himself he would donate ten times more in the next year's *himmet* meeting.[102] He adds that he asked God in his prayers to help him fulfill his promise. However, Akif Bey recommended that he donate an amount of *himmet* five times more than what he had in mind. Asılsoy recounts, "Thank God! I was able to pay my annual *himmet,* which was about five times more than that of the previous year, in the two months following the *himmet* meeting."[103] Erhan Bey, who participated in this *himmet* meeting, mentions the "passion for giving" that he observed in the *himmet* meetings in Gaziantep as the main motivating factor for him.[104] Over time, these meetings became standardized as annual *himmet* meetings in which participants would pledge their annual donations. Yet, they have also remained a tool that is utilized in case of financial crisis.

THE ISSUE OF ACCOUNTABILITY

Who monitors the flow of donations and whether the funds are spent wisely? The operational structure of the movement is designed to minimize any likely mismanagement of the funds collected and suspicions in that regard. Firstly, all of the decisions regarding a service project are taken by a group of people who are in charge of the project in question. The individuals in the *istişare* group are also those who procure the funds both by donating on their own and by seeking other donors. Therefore, they become automatically alert to any misuse of the funds. Orhan Tutkun, general manager of a group of Gülen-inspired schools in Mardin, explains, "The managing board of the company that runs all these educational institutions in Mardin consists of local Mardin people who are also the most prominent donors." He stresses that the local people who donate in the *himmet* meetings are knowledgeable about the status of the ongoing projects at any given time, for they are personally responsible for many of them. Therefore, it is quite easy for them to monitor how the received donations are used. Tutkun adds, "The donors mostly feel obliged to seek other donors upon realizing that the donations already accumulated are not sufficient to complete the project in hand."[105] On this issue, Vahit Atak has a pragmatic approach, saying, "Seventy percent is a good return on an investment. I was initially cautious about where the money goes. Seeing well-educated graduates of these schools is worth every dollar I donate, even if some thirty percent of it might be wasted due to likely mismanagement." He adds, "Also, I do not believe that the teachers and administrators of these schools would steal the donations. After all, if they were interested in money, they would not come to Mardin for sure."[106]

It seems that the project groups in the movement have sought to maintain transparency in financial issues by charging a group of donors, instead of an individual, with both procuring and allocating the funds. Since most donors are somehow involved in the project for which the donations are being pledged, they monitor the flow of donations and check on whether they are spent wisely. This group (instead of individual) monitoring of funds does not necessarily rule out the possibility of mismanaging the funds, but it does seem to minimize it. For those projects in which the donors have no direct involvement, information is available in the *istişare* meetings, as those who attend these meetings discuss not only new projects, but also those that are ongoing.[107]

THINKING BIG

Thinking big and the consequent need for more funds to establish more university preparatory courses led the Mardin *mütevelli* (board of trustees) of the Gülen-inspired schools to larger cities, such as Istanbul, Izmir, and Ankara. The increasing number of the students in the first university preparatory course made it necessary to establish a second one that could hold more students. Ibrahim Bey, the project coordinator who succeeded Akif Bey, proposed that the *mütevelli* contact Mardinian businessmen and other wealthy people living in the large cities in order to seek their financial support for ongoing and future education projects in Mardin. During a visit with wealthy Mardinians, a businessman in Istanbul donated the land which would be used for the current university preparatory course building in downtown Mardin. In cooperation with their counterparts in Istanbul and other large cities, the Mardin *mütevelli* reached out to both Mardinian and non-Mardinian businessmen and sought their contributions, either in cash or supplies.

Some businessmen, especially small- and medium-size manufacturers, have donated their own products (e.g., furniture, construction material or school appliances), which has made the procurement and mobility of resources proceed faster. Hayri Bey of the Mardin *mütevelli* notes that they collected truckloads of furniture and appliances on most of these trips.[108] Another significant contribution has come from Ankara, the capital city of Turkey. In 1996, the establishment of the new university preparatory course was disrupted again because the funds that had been collected from the people in the Mardin *sohbet* groups had all been spent.[109] Asılsoy notes that in the *himmet* meeting held prior to building the downtown facility for the university preparatory course several people donated both money and their cars.[110] Nevertheless, new funds were still needed. Malik Bey, the project coordinator who succeeded Ibrahim Bey, proposed visiting wealthy Mardinians in the larger cities again. Malik Bey, Asılsoy, and several other people in the Mardin *mütevelli* visited Ismail Bölükbaşı, a wealthy Mardinian businessman in Ankara who owns a chain of gas stations, in order to solicit about five billion Turkish lira (approximately twenty-five thousand US dollars). They explained the situation back home and expressed the need to complete ongoing projects. To their great surprise, notes Asılsoy, Ismail Bölükbaşı promised to donate three times the amount they had asked for every month.[111] Similar examples of 'giving' have followed, one after the other, as a result of other visits to wealthy Mardinians.

At this point, one could argue that the Gülen movement has brought the concept of *vakıf* (charitable trust), which was utilized during the Ottoman era, back into daily life in a modernized fashion.[112] The experience of the Mardin *mütevelli* demonstrated that the ordinary people they contacted, whether rich or not, were all eager to donate for a cause that they thought would be beneficial for the common good. Moreover, Gülen and people inspired by him have mobilized idle resources, not for building larger and modernized mosques, but for building modern schools that follow officially endorsed, secular curricula. In that regard, the movement's development of education facilities in Mardin has been made possible largely by mobilizing idle resources from elsewhere.

Those the Mardin *mütevelli* contacted in the larger cities were mostly aware of the Gülen movement and its education campaign, so it was not difficult for the Mardin *mütevelli* to procure resources from them. In addition to sharing the vision of the Gülen movement participants with the Mardin *mütevelli*, the non-Mardinian contributors helped establish Mardin's education facilities out of a sense of contributing to the development of one of their country's least-developed and most problematic areas.

THE FIRST PRIVATE SCHOOL: "TEACH THEM TO FISH ..."

The idea of opening a private school—in fact, the first and only private school—in Mardin came about during one of the Mardin *mütevelli*'s trips to Istanbul in 1995. The wealthy Mardinians living there advised the Mardin *mütevelli* to contact the Atak family.[113] During their visit with the family, the Mardin *mütevelli* explained the situation of Mardin's education projects and invited the family to see the projects on site. Dr. Vahit Atak, owner of a private hospital and several shoe factories, expressed his family's desire to do something for their impoverished hometown. He suggested that they build a public bakery to distribute free bread to Mardin's poor people every day.[114] In response, Ibrahim Bey, the project coordinator at that time, suggested that this would be like feeding the poor people a fish every day. He then asked why they did not teach the poor people how to fish, that is, provide them with the skills needed to earn their bread every day.[115] Mahmut, Vahit Atak's brother, was initially opposed to what he thought were the vision and activities of the movement and, according to Vahit, thought that the Gülen movement was a religious movement that was deceiving people and sought, as its ultimate goal, to establish an Islamic state. Nevertheless, the Mardin *mütevelli* convinced the Atak brothers to visit Mardin.

This visit not only changed their idea about what should be done for the poor in Mardin, but also about the educational vision of the Gülen movement. The most striking experience for them was seeing the teachers constructing the building that would house the university preparatory courses. Vahit Atak mentions how he was ashamed to see teachers sacrificing their time and energy for his hometown, "After all, none of these teachers was from Mardin or from southeastern Turkey for that matter. They had all graduated from good universities and could have made good money elsewhere." He continues, "Yet, they came to Mardin, where socio-economic deprivation was at its peak and security was not guaranteed because of the PKK terror in the early 1990s."[116]

On the same trip, they witnessed similar scenes in each province of Mardin. In Midyat, recalls Vahit Atak, they saw a half-finished and disrupted university preparatory course building that could not be continued because of a lack of funds. By the end of this trip, realizing that the current number of university preparatory courses was not meeting the demand in Mardin and that the number of applicants was increasing, the Atak brothers decided to build a school instead of a bakery. Seeing the actual need on the ground, what had been done to meet that need, and that the number of Mardinian students eligible for university increased dramatically after the university preparatory courses were established, they made up their minds. Also, unlike his brother, Vahit Atak already knew about the Gülen movement and had visited several of the schools. Therefore, he knew what to expect as a return on his investment. This pre-knowledge expedited the realization of the private school idea.

The way Vahit Atak adopted the *hizmet* discourse illustrates the general pattern of how the movement has mobilized resources and expanded the field of its activities. Long before meeting the Mardin *mütevelli*, Vahit Atak had heard about the Gülen movement and its educational vision in Istanbul from a 1988 conversation with his neighbor. Ever since then, he had participated in the *sohbet*s in which Gülen's educational vision was always one of the main topics. Moreover, he was already contributing to the educational activities by giving scholarships to poor students in Gülen-inspired schools. He had also joined several trips to the Fatih and Yamanlar high schools. He had formed a good impression of the education system in these schools, a secular education system strengthened with universal ethical values displayed in the teachers' attitudes, as Vahit Atak puts it. He notes that he had observed quite an improvement in the manners of his extended family's children who were students at Fatih High School.

In addition, during his visit to Yamanlar High School, Vahit Atak had attended one of Gülen's public addresses where Gülen had urged the audience to build schools. After that, Vahit Atak stresses, he started to consider building a school as an option. The Mardin *mütevelli*'s visit to the Atak family coincidentally took place in the days following Vahit Atak's visit to Yamanlar High School. Therefore, he did not resist the Mardin *mütevelli*'s request to build a school identical to the Fatih and Yamanlar high schools.

The process that started with Vahit Atak's first encounter with participants in the Gülen movement in a *sohbet* meeting and eventually resulted in his decision to build a school in

Mardin has repeated itself, with different actors, in most of the places that now have a Gülen-inspired school. Therefore, one can conclude that the *sohbet* meetings are a sort of public sphere that communicates the educational vision of the Gülen movement to more and more people and that, consequently, meeting participants, depending on their capacities, have contributed to realizing that vision.

THE PROLIFERATION OF *SOHBET* GROUPS

The *sohbet* meetings have been the main tool in reaching out to more and more individuals and sharing the Gülen movement's educational vision.[117] They have constituted the pool of individuals out of which the *mütevelli* groups, which have felt more responsible for carrying out the education projects, have been formed.

This process is evident in the development of the activities of the Gülen movement in Mardin. It started in 1988 with conversations over tea with several local people in which such general themes as the need for educational facilities and the problem of youth unemployment and its contribution to increased support for both PKK and Hizbullah were discussed. These conversations gradually assumed a more organized form through the participants' collective decision making that then brought the education project of the Gülen movement to fruition in Mardin first, and then in many different Turkish cities.

The participants in the first Mardin *sohbet* group, Fatih Asılsoy, Hayri Bey, Davut Bey, and a few others, felt responsible for completing those education projects and therefore traveled to larger cities to seek funds and physically helped build the facility for the university preparatory courses if needed. Basically, they moved on from the *sohbet* meetings and became *mütevelli* members by willingly taking on direct and indirect responsibilities. Through a similar process, Vahit Atak has become a *mütevelli* member in Istanbul. He learned about the educational vision of the Gülen movement through the *sohbet* meetings in which he participated at his neighbor's invitation. As he notes, he serves in the Mardin *mütevelli* on a voluntary basis and tries to develop that town's education infrastructure.[118] Thus, for both the Mardin group and Vahit Atak, the process of becoming a *mütevelli* member and assuming more responsibility started with the *sohbet* meetings. That is to say, the individuals in the *sohbet* groups, depending on their personal preference, may or may not take on more responsibility. This does not necessarily require more financial capacity, but more individual dedication.

This process is intact in Mardin today. The Gülen movement volunteers continue to use the *sohbet* meetings as a means to communicate their educational vision to more people in Mardin. As the movement has reached more people and the number of the *sohbet* groups has increased, these meetings have become more homogeneous in terms of the participants' social characteristics. The main purpose of this seems to be the idea of increasing commonalities among the *sohbet* participants. These commonalities are based on the participants' similarities in profession and residential proximity so that they can better connect with each other and continue their dialogue outside the *sohbet* meetings. Otherwise, the groups are not based on the participants' socio-economic status or ethnicity.

Mardin's *sohbet* groups have been categorized mainly according to the participants' professions: doctors, teachers, workers, civil servants, imams, and so on. I participated in a doctors' *sohbet* meeting, which was basically a social event for civil servants in the health-care sector.[119] The event included a dinner and tea conversation in which the main themes were the shortcomings of the local health-care system, the difficulties of working in this sector, and what could be done to improve the conditions. One participant stated that the meetings are quite refreshing for him after a week of heavy work in the hospital, and that they provide an opportunity for him to see friends he would normally not see, since everyone has a busy schedule.

The *sohbet* meetings include a short discussion session following a reading of part of a book either by Gülen or by another author. The books or articles read usually emphasize the values of the *hizmet* discourse: altruism, giving with no expectation of return, self-sacrifice for the common good, piety, and self-criticism. Murat Bey of Kızıltepe, organizer of the imams' *sohbet* meeting, notes that there has been a substantial change in many imams' ideas since they started to participate, "Some imams who more or less have some affinity with Hizbullah and approve radicalism initially had a problem with the Gülen movement's educational vision and questioned why the movement is not taking up arms or establishing a political party. ...After several *sohbet* meetings in which they acquainted themselves with the Sufi interpretation of Islam in Gülen's writings, their views in favor of the use of violence in the name of religion have been minimized, if not eradicated."[120] Therefore, the *sohbet* meetings have had a moderating effect on those imams.

The Gülen movement does not seem to be a male-dominated movement. Every activity from *sohbet* meetings to *mütev-*

elli groups is held among women as well.[121] The ethno-religious identities of the women vary greatly and include Turks, Kurds, Arabs, and Assyrian Christians.[122] A history teacher in Atak High School notes that "the *sohbet* meetings and other social activities, such as the breakfast and dinner events, constitute our main tools to communicate with our students' parents."[123] She states that at least once a week, the mothers of the Atak High School students as well as their friends, who are not necessarily related to the high school, get together in the *sohbet* meetings to discuss and set an agenda to reach out to more women and get them involved in their activities. The most notable of these activities are reading competitions and group visits to villages; distributing food, clothes, and books in these villages; and trying to convince parents in the villages to send their daughters to school. She emphasizes, "The parents in the rural areas are quite sensitive about their daughters going to school and losing their morality. Seeing us as a role model, they trust us and are easily convinced to send their daughters to school."[124] In addition, she explains that every month the women organize a reading competition, encourage each other to read as many books of their choice as possible, and reward the winner at the end of the month. Like the men's meetings, the women's meetings constitute the pool of individuals from which the *mütevelli* groups are formed. "Some of the women," explains the history teacher, "like to be more involved in organizing events and take on more responsibility, so they become the members of a *mütevelli* group, which requires more time, effort, and dedication."[125]

One of the most critical questions about these meetings is the following: What is it about the *sohbet* meetings that brings people together? By the same token, what is it about them that prevents the *sohbet* groups from dissolving as a result of the likely differences of opinion among the participants? First, it seems there are several issues, as opposed to just one, that might appeal to the participants. Based on my interviews with participants, I conclude that some joined to socialize with people who have common interests, such as the same profession or living in the same neighborhood; for some, it was the teaching aspect, as well as the reading and discussion sessions; for others, it was the Sufi interpretation and practice of Islam taught in Gülen's writings; and, finally, for some, it was the education campaign of the movement. This last group of participants seems to be more dedicated and involved in organizing activities and carrying out the education projects. They not only donate but also seek donations from their friends and relatives. In this way, still being a part of the general *sohbet* groups, they naturally form the local *mütevelli* groups.

In the next chapter, I will examine the institutions and their activities that have come into being as the result of the diffusion of the movement in Mardin. These institutions include the Sur university preparatory courses, Atak High School, and the reading halls.

5

Gülen-inspired Institutions in Mardin

SUR DERSANESI: UNIVERSITY PREPARATORY COURSES

Sur Dersanesi is a pioneer in Mardin in preparing the local youth for the national university entrance exam. Before Sur Dersanesi, a few organizations had attempted to run university preparatory courses in Mardin. However, they had ceased their operations either because of financial hardship or the security problems caused by the PKK and Hizbullah in the 1980s. In other words, they fled Mardin without fulfilling their promises to the local people to prepare their children for the national university entrance test.[126] This unfortunate precedent initially made it difficult for the local participants in the movement to obtain the necessary official endorsement from the local government.

In 1992, Mardin participants in the Gülen movement succeeded in opening their first university preparatory course, which was also their first local institution. Ever since then, the expansion of the movement in Mardin has been focused on opening university preparatory courses. Currently, the volunteers run four university preparatory courses in the surrounding counties of Kızıltepe, Derik, Nusaybin, and Midyat. These courses serve the students not only in their own counties but also in nearby counties. For instance, since there is no university preparatory course in Dargeçit yet, students commute to the closest county (Midyat) to attend the course. Opening another branch of Sur Dersanesi is always one of the top items on the agenda of the *mütevelli* in Mardin. In that regard, Mardin's *mütevelli* is currently negotiating with the local authorities of Savur, another county in Mardin, to obtain a license and rent a building to open a university preparatory course there.

The growth of Sur Dersanesi in Nusaybin is similar to that of its branches in the other counties. According to Murat Salim, a local store owner and resident of Nusaybin, the city has been heavily influenced by both the PKK and Hizbullah: "Between 1989 and 1993, the region was under the complete control of the PKK. For instance, if there was an incident that required a judicial process, the parties had to first see the regional administrator of the PKK. If they went directly to the official court, then the PKK punished them for that wrongdoing."[127] He suggests that Hizbullah, the counter-guerilla group, took over control of Nusaybin from the PKK after 1993. About this time, Gülen movement participants opened a first university preparatory course in Nusaybin. Murat Salim notes, "Sur Dersanesi in Nusaybin had about ten to fifteen students in 1996, but the number of the students has grown every year. The number was 280 in 2004, 480 in 2005, and 900 in 2006."[128]

This growth has mirrored the growth in the other counties, such as Kızıltepe and Derik, which are under heavy PKK influence. Fatih Asılsoy, a local businessman in Mardin, recalls that he and Akif Bey, coordinator of the education projects, had to look for a rental building to open the first university preparatory course in Kızıltepe in 1994 while most of the stores were forced by the PKK to shut down during the day time.[129] Today, even though Kızıltepe is still a PKK stronghold, the local people send their children to Sur Dersanesi.

The educational vision of Gülen and the movement participants appeals to the citizens of Mardin for various reasons. For the local people who are not necessarily attracted to the movement's emphasis on moral values,[130] these schools and university preparatory courses are mere service providers that will educate their children in modern facilities that no other school in Mardin can match. For those who are sensitive about moral values, the Gülen-inspired institutions are places where their children will receive the education necessary for their career, as well as adopt Islam's ethical values. Several respondents I interviewed, who would fall into the latter group, noted that they sent their children because the teachers at the school are practicing Muslims and do not have such bad habits as smoking or drinking alcohol that could negatively influence their children.

In fact, religious piety and the avoidance of smoking, drinking, and other harmful habits are the main characteristics associated with any individual who is actively involved with the Gülen movement. Therefore, this general public perception about the emphasis on Islam's moral values makes the Gülen-inspired schools appeal to the Mardinians who prioritize those moral values. However, the teachers' habits are the reason some other parents do *not* send their children to the Gülen movement schools. "The teachers do not proselytize or teach religion to the students," says one parent, "but they dress so well and behave towards students in such a friendly way that my daughters were taking them as a role model… [but] I know that there is no better school to which I can send my daughters."[131]

So, the reason for supporting the movement varies from the merely utilitarian to sharing a similar moral outlook. However, the mere fact that a majority of Mardinians, regardless of their political views, support the educational vision of the movement in its presence in their county or city shows that the Gülen movement has been able to appeal to various segments of Mardin society by addressing their common needs and providing solid services to meet those needs.

Atak Koleji: Elementary and Secondary High Schools

Atak Koleji is the first and so far the only private school in Mardin. Its construction, which is still ongoing, started in 1996. In the meantime, however, the school has registered students and provided an education. The construction of the school has been funded solely by a wealthy Mardinian family (the Ataks) that has been residing in Istanbul since 1974. The family decided to build the school upon the encouragement of a group of Mardin's local businessmen and a teacher who share Gülen's educational vision and believe that increased educational facilities are the only remedy for Mardin's underdevelopment and the way to solve southeastern Turkey's terrorism problem. When the Atak family visited Mardin and saw that non-Mardinian teachers, despite all the deprivations they suffered there, were dedicating themselves to educating Mardin's children and youth at the university preparatory courses, the family was stimulated to contribute to the Gülen-inspired educational projects in Mardin. They are still contributing.[132]

Just as it is the first institution in Mardin to be funded solely by a civic initiative, Atak Koleji is the first in terms of other characteristics. It has become a meeting place for the area's different ethno-religious groups, most notably Kurds and Arabs. The school is located halfway between Kızıltepe (Mardin's largest county) and the city center of Mardin, which are, respectively, strongholds of ethnic Kurdish and ethnic Arab populations. According to reports made by Atak Koleji teachers, even if the Kurds and Arabs have not engaged in a visible conflict, they have not quite intermingled either.[133] As a result, they report, there are elderly ethnic Kurds in Kızıltepe who have never stepped in the Arab-populated city center of Mardin and vice versa. In addition to Kurdish and Arab students, the school also has Assyrian Christian students. It follows a secular curriculum approved (and periodically inspected) by the Turkish Ministry of Education. Atak Koleji is a co-ed school and has about three hundred and fifty students taught by thirty teachers, fourteen of whom are women.[134] This student diversity exemplifies the main thesis of this research: the education projects of the Gülen movement are able to bring together very different segments of society by addressing and providing solid services for the common needs of each segment. Especially in today's Turkey, where DEHAP (The Democratic People's Party) is perceived as the political wing of the separatist PKK organization, it is remarkable to see that Atak Koleji has been able to gain the trust of and therefore enroll the children of DEHAP's most notable figures.

THE ATAK DIFFERENCE

The school is unique in Mardin for its education system and the opportunities it provides to its students. Like the Fatih, Yamanlar, and Samanyolu high schools,[135] Atak Koleji in Mardin prepares its students intensively for international science contests and for the national university entrance and placement test that every high school graduate has to pass in order to attend a university. Along with the natural sciences (e.g., physics and chemistry) and math, English as a second language and computer science are also taught at much higher levels than they are at the city's public schools. In fact, the majority of the public schools lack teachers for such basic courses as math and physics, let alone English as a second language and computer science; Atak Koleji, on the other hand, provides students with opportunities to set up their own clubs for English, computer science, physics, and other subjects. The school achieved a ninety-five percent success rate in the university entrance and placement test last year. Eighteen out of nineteen graduates passed the test, and nine out of the eighteen were able to enter medical school. The local people's passion for medical school has made Atak Koleji even more popular since half of its graduates were admitted to prominent medical schools.

The school prioritizes its students' development in terms not only of academic skills, but also of social and physical skills. Throughout the year, the students organize science fairs, exhibitions, theater plays, music performances, chess tournaments, and such sporting events as soccer and basketball tournaments. The teachers encourage each student club to organize its own events and participate in those of the other clubs. The school principal Oğuz Ozan explains, "At the end of every school year, a fair is held among the student clubs; these clubs present the activities and accomplishments they have achieved in that year. The local people are invited to the fair and are asked to vote for the best clubs. The students are free to invite as many people as possible, including those with no affiliation to the school, in order to increase the number of votes for their club. Last year, the students brought about five thousand people from the city to visit the fair, and sought to increase the number of their votes."[136] Ozan believes that this voting application helps familiarize students with democratic election practices.

Similarly, Atak Koleji encourages student clubs to be as active as possible not only within the school campus, but all over Mardin. The villages' reforestation activities constitute the main portion of the contribution of the student clubs to the city. In cooperation with MARKOYDER (Mardin Village Development Association), the student clubs contact the administrator (*muhtar*) of a village and set a date for planting trees in the village, which is heavily deforested. MARKOY-DER provides the plants, and the students of Atak Koleji plant them in partnership with the residents of the chosen village. In fact, the students become the mobilizing factor and the villagers do the planting. After this activity, the village residents undertake to continue the planting in the rest of their deforested fields.

ATAK KOLEJI IN PUBLIC

Most of the student club activities involve public participation. However, Atak Koleji also holds events and activities throughout the year that are specifically designed to educate students' parents and local people about the need for more educational facilities in Mardin. These include public seminars, literacy courses, social gatherings, and dinner events.

Principal Ozan states that they try to use every opportunity to be in contact with parents. In this regard, they hold periodic "Sunday Breakfast on Campus" events to get together with their students' parents; they go on picnics together; and they hold frequent teacher-parent meetings to discuss the children's current situations. Through these informal social gatherings, notes Ozan, the school maintains strong relations with parents and makes them feel responsible for their children's development. In this way, the school shares responsibility with the parents to better educate the students.

Moreover, the school organizes public seminars that are followed by dinner events. Through these public seminars, the school shares its vision and future projects with the local people and seeks their contributions. The contributions come in the form of individual donations, registering their children for school, and personally being involved in carrying out the projects. The goal of these public seminars does not seem to be to convince the local people to send their children to Atak Koleji; rather, it is to convince them to send their children to any school. In fact, the tuition fees mean that only parents with enough money can register a child at Atak Koleji, unless the child is awarded a scholarship by the school.[137] In encouraging the local people to send their children to any school, the ultimate goal is to overcome the indigenous parental traditions of not sending their sons to school after a certain age and of not sending their daughters to school at all.

In addition to public seminars on campus, school teachers organize field trips to the villages in cooperation with MARKOYDER and seek to convince those parents who do not attend these seminars to send their children to school. This approach has been quite effective, especially in increasing the number of girls attending school. When the female teachers of Atak Koleji talk with the parents, they are examples of what their daughters might become if they are educated. In other words, when parents meet with female teachers who observe their religious duties and yet are modern, well-educated, and self-confident, they are easily convinced to send their daughters to school. Mothers in villages, especially, have become more enthusiastic about sending their daughters to school, upon meeting female teachers of Atak Koleji, since they themselves have never had the chance to go to school and, as a result, have experienced many deprivations.

A mother from Surgucu village laments, "I was not allowed to go even to elementary school and was married at a very early age." She continues, "I did not have much say in my immediate family, let alone the extended one, but I am quite happy for Hatice [her daughter] because she is going to high school now in Balıkesir [a western city]. Even now, her father consults her for her ideas on issues. She has the opportunity to influence her father's decisions. She will be a strong woman and a good mother."[138] Hayri Serhat of Kızıltepe, father to three daughters, two of whom are attending university to become a medical doctor and a school teacher respectively, and one of whom is preparing for the university entrance exam, says, "In Mardin, especially in rural areas, parents are willing not to send their daughters to school at all if they are doubtful about moral and security conditions at the school. ...Now most of them send their daughters to the courses and to Atak Koleji because they see the female teachers in these institutions as role models for their daughters."[139] Thus, the university preparatory courses and Atak Koleji have been effective in increasing the number of rural girls from Mardin attending school.

In addition, the school educates parents through literacy courses and by encouraging them to get involved in student club activities. The teachers at the school make extra time throughout the year for free public literacy courses in order to raise the literacy rate in the city.[140] Local women attend the classes on campus and learn how to read and write. For parents who are already literate, the school designs activities to encourage reading. Principal Ozan mentions a "Twenty Minutes' Reading a Day" program that Atak Koleji has applied on campus. According to the program, every day at a certain time all teachers, students, and support personnel in the school stop whatever they are doing and read a book of their own choice for the next twenty minutes while listening to music in the background. Ozan states that they wanted to involve the students' parents in the reading program as well. They therefore held a seminar on campus to communicate how important parental involvement in the reading program is to encouraging the students to read more. The school rewards the parents who have read the most books at the end of the school year at the students' graduation ceremony.

Finally, as a part of its public relations, Atak Koleji holds frequent dinner events for different professional groups throughout the year. The school has hosted lawyers, medical doctors, civil servants, workers, and other professional groups at these dinner events. Through these events, the school has sought to increase the participants' awareness of the necessity for more education facilities and to get them to contribute to the educational projects. In this way, they have shared the educational vision of the Gülen movement in Mardin.

The school has also organized field trips to surrounding cities for the people they have hosted on campus. The purpose of these trips, according to Atak Koleji's teachers, is to show the practical results of the educational vision that they have discussed in the public seminars. During these recreational trips, they also visit the Gülen-inspired schools in these cities. Atak Koleji has been so active in public relations and has held so many dinner events that the local people jokingly call it "Atak Restaurant."[141]

MARKOYDER AND MOSDER

MARKOYDER (Mardin Village Development Association) and MOSDER (Mardin Reading Halls Association) are civic, non-governmental organizations which were established by individuals inspired by the Gülen movement, and which seek to provide educational services to Mardin's rural areas. Both organizations were founded in 2004 and operate in cooperation with each other and Atak Koleji. MOSDER's emphasis is, by definition, on opening reading halls in the impoverished rural areas, where there are no university preparatory courses despite the sizeable student population. The main objective of the reading halls, as Şükrü Bey, the administrator of Dargeçit's reading hall puts it, is to provide books and media so that young people who are not able to pay for the university preparatory course can prepare individually for the national university entrance exam and, if not old enough to go to university yet, can spend time reading instead of wasting it on the streets.[142] MARKOYDER has a larger scope: it makes contact with villages through village administrators or the village mosque imams, identifies the village's needs, and seeks resources to meet those needs.

MOSDER

MOSDER has several branches in Mardin, one of which is in the highly impoverished and isolated Dargeçit province. Dargeçit does not have a bank, despite its more than seven thousand inhabitants, and has one entrance, which also serves as an exit and a military checkpoint. The main reason for such deprivation and heavy military control seems to be a combination of the local people's implicit support for the PKK, frequent clashes between the PKK and the Turkish security forces in the vicinity of Dargeçit, Ankara's neglect when it comes to developing Dargeçit, and the resulting absence of investment. MOSDER's reading hall opened in February 2005 and serves about one hundred and fifty students. The students are encouraged to spend as much time as possible there reading or studying for the national university admissions test. The students stress that the reading hall has helped them organize their preparation for the university admissions test by providing them with a study place and test books, and that without these they would not be able to prepare very well in their poor and crowded houses. In terms of procuring the testing materials and books, MOSDER cooperates with both Atak Koleji and Sur university preparatory courses in Mardin.

MARKOYDER

Compared to MOSDER, MARKOYDER has a more comprehensive scope for its activities, from providing educational facilities to distributing food and clothing to poor villagers. The operational relation between the two organizations is such that MOSDER goes into a village if MARKOYDER identifies a need for a reading hall in that village, and they cooperate in opening the reading hall. In addition, MARKOYDER, in partnership with the teachers from Atak Koleji, visits families in the villages and tries to convince parents to send their children to school, especially their daughters, since the indigenous conservative culture impedes girls from going to school. Fethi Bey, the head of MARKOYDER, reports that they have been in contact with more than a hundred villages so far.

MARKOYDER and Atak Koleji also work together in rural reforestation activities. MARKOYDER identifies deforested villages and procures the necessary number of plants from the relevant public institutions. Then, the students and teachers from Atak Koleji and the people of the local villages plant the saplings. MARKOYDER also provides food aid to the villages as part of its portfolio of activities. The main food distribution takes place during and after Kurban Bayram, the three-day Muslim festival, when every Muslim that can afford to do so sacrifices a sheep or a cow and donates two-thirds of the meat. MARKOYDER collects meat donations from Mardin and other Turkish cities and then distributes the meat to the poor villagers. First, such solid and immediate services in neglected areas gain public trust for the projects and services by the people inspired by Fethullah Gülen. Second, when the local Kurdish villagers see the mostly non-Kurdish teachers distributing this aid, be it food or clothing, which has been donated by mostly non-Kurdish people living in other cities of Turkey, it lowers—if not totally eradicates—the impact of the idea of an "inherent Kurdish–Turkish" conflict.

One may not conclude that these activities, all of which cause Turks, Kurds, and Arabs to intermingle, have caused overall popular support in the area for either the PKK or Hizbullah to decline. However, one may conclude from the interviews with local recipients of the donations as well as local participants in the activities, who sometimes may be the same people, that the greater the local people's involvement with the Gülen movement, the less affinity they have for either the PKK or Hizbullah. This change contributes to understanding why the local people accept the movement and, similarly, why the movement is popular in Mardin.

MARKOYDER's *sohbet* meetings with the imams have been instrumental in lowering popular support in the area for Hizbullah and for radical Islamist groups. A local Mardinian notes, "There are about forty to fifty unofficial religious schools in and around Mardin. The state does not allow them to operate." These unofficial religious schools train imams that are relatively closer to radical Islamist groups like Hizbullah and al-Qaeda. MARKOYDER's *sohbet* meetings with the imams, some of whom have radical tendencies, focus mostly on the moderate interpretation of Qur'anic texts. Hasan Bey, a local Mardinian who organizes these meetings, emphasizes the moderating effect of these *sohbet*s on the imams. Abdulbari Hodja, an imam in Nusaybin, declares that the *hizmet* culture provided by the Gülen movement has substantially changed his outlook on being a pious Muslim.[143]

WHAT GÜLEN-INSPIRED INSTITUTIONS MEAN TO LOCALS

According to my interviewees' responses, Atak Koleji seems to be matchless in Mardin in terms of the education it provides the students. Similarly, Sur Dersanesi, the university preparatory courses, and the reading halls seem to provide the locals with opportunities that the state cannot offer and that perhaps only a small percentage of Mardinians could afford on their own. The material value of these services is clear. However, the local people also seem to attribute a special meaning to these institutions, for they view them as being more than just schools. There are contextual reasons for this special meaning: the local realities of severe unemployment, terror, a conservative culture, and a chronic shortage of schools and teachers. These correspond almost perfectly with what Atak Koleji and the university preparatory courses are committed to eradicating. Therefore, the fact that each of these contextual reasons is important to the parents, although to varying degrees, makes Atak Koleji, as well as the other Gülen-inspired educational institutions, something more than what such institutions, by common definition, are.

The local people who have placed their children in these institutions comment that they see the Gülen-inspired institutions as a way of enabling their children to resist the influence of both the PKK and Hizbullah. Although they do not reflect the entire Mardin community, those parents who send their children to the university preparatory course view it as a way to rescue their children from the recruitment pool of both the PKK and Hizbullah. Based on this proposition, one cannot argue that the movement's activities have decreased local support for the PKK and Hizbullah, but we can conclude, based on the parents' statements, that their main motivation is not necessarily to help their children go to university but to keep them away from the streets, which constitutes the main recruitment pool for both the PKK and Hizbullah. Moreover, the increasing number of students in Sur Dersanesi in all branches indicates that those who pass the national university admissions test set an example for the students that will take the test the following year. These repeated successes also increase the popularity of Sur Dersanesi, as well as of other institutions established by Gülen movement participants.

Aside from their educational success, Gülen's popularity among the local people contributes to the popular support for these institutions. This may not be the main factor for choosing the Gülen-inspired institutions, but it apparently is a secondary reason for the locals' trust in them. Oğuz Ozan, the principal of Atak Koleji, recounts, "An Assyrian Christian couple was initially hesitant to register their child for a school where the student body was predominantly Muslim but felt comfortable when they learned that the school had been established by the local Mardinians who follow the teachings of Fethullah Gülen."[144] So, there is a variety of reasons for the local people to support the activities of the movement in Mardin. According to my interviews with the locals, people support the educational vision of Gülen and the movement because they see in it an antidote to the terror problem, or because they want their children to have a better future, or because the Gülen-inspired institutions are seen as tolerant and open to everyone. These widespread comments may not account for the overall decrease in popular support for the PKK and Hizbullah in the city. However, based on my interviews, I argue that the emergence and development of the movement has caused local people whose children have been educated in these institutions to reduce their support for both the PKK and Hizbullah.

6

Conclusion

The spread of the Gülen movement throughout the world is not something one would expect during the "War on Terror" and strict scrutiny of every collective action that has an Islamic element to it. Yet, the Gülen movement, which started in Turkey in the late 1960s as a non-political, faith-based civic movement, has established itself in over ninety countries and built more than five hundred educational and cultural institutions. These countries are not only Turkic or Muslim, as many would expect, but also secular Western countries. Most interestingly, the movement's transnational spread has been carried out in only fourteen years (1992–2006), while it took about three decades for the movement to mature in Turkey to undertake such a global outreach.

The question is: What enables the Gülen movement to diffuse into so many different societies in such a short period of time? In this vein, the essential research questions answered by this study are: How does the Gülen movement diffuse? What is its mechanism of diffusion? I found it appropriate to complement this main research question with a relevant secondary question: What are the factors behind the popular support for the movement? That is, why do people welcome the activities of the Gülen movement? The aim of this second and complementary question was to eliminate the notion of illegality or clandestineness implicit in the concept of "diffusion," especially when it is about diffusion of a social movement. One may suggest that in doing so I may have breached the investigator's objectivity toward the subject being studied by presuming that the movement is both popular and non-clandestine. I contend that in doing so, I have only sought to accurately reflect the status of the subject studied. In fact, the evidence that the movement has been operational in more than ninety countries and that it has apparently been monitored by local authorities and has never been accused of carrying out any illegal activities supports the transparent nature of the movement.

The scholarly studies on the Gülen movement have been quite limited in number and in content. First, there has not been a substantial amount of academic work based on field research. Second, no study has sought to model the mechanism of the Gülen movement's diffusion into a wide variety of communities that differ from each other greatly in terms of culture, political system, and ethno-religious identity. What I have tried to do with this study is to address the issue of the movement's diffusion mechanism. I chose Mardin as a sample of the broad geographical area throughout which the movement operates. Then, I examined the historical development of the movement's activities in the city after 1988, when a participant in the movement shared the vision of Gülen and the movement with a local person and discussed whether together they could achieve that vision in Mardin.

Scholars of both religious and social movement studies, most notably Zeki Sarıtoprak, Sidney Griffith, Osman Bakar, and Thomas Michel have studied Fethullah Gülen's ideas and his views on such contemporary debates as modernity versus tradition, science versus religion, and secularism versus Islam. In much of this research, Gülen has been central to studies about the Gülen movement. That is, these academic studies have mainly focused on him and scrutinized his views on the contemporary debates of modernity versus tradition, science versus religion, and Islam versus secularism. Similarly, in the few studies that examine the educational institutions that the participants of the movement have opened across the world, again Gülen's views on education and how they are put into practice are examined. However, academic studies seeking to explain the movement's successful spread into different cultures have been almost completely absent.

In fact, the diffusion of social movements in general has rarely been studied compared to other topics in social movement studies. Scholars utilizing the theory of diffusion have confined themselves mainly to explaining the spread of political practices and scientific techniques. Doug McAdam and Dieter Rucht, however, for the first time employed the theory of diffusion to explain the spread of social movements into non-familiar communities. McAdam and Rucht argued that different social movements operating in two or more countries can learn about and adopt each other's values, ideas, and visions through relational and non-relational channels, and that, in this way, such communication enables one social movement to diffuse into another society. Relational channels consist of such interpersonal relations as meetings and one-to-one discussions. Once that initial contact has been established, such non-relational channels as media and literature maintain and strengthen the communication between those social movements. Put simply, the diffusing social movement acts as transmitter and the adopting social movement acts as receiver. The interaction between the two consists of a transfer of vision, ideas, values and practices as a message from the former to the latter. In proportion to the efficiency of such interaction, the former's social movement diffuses into the latter's community.

Doug McAdam and Dieter Rucht's theory of diffusion proves useful in explaining the diffusion of the Gülen movement. The Gülen movement participants enter a new community through its activists' personal contact with the local people. Those initial contacts, during which the activists find an opportunity to introduce their vision and seek the local people's cooperation, produce tangible outcomes such as establishing schools and cultural houses in partnership with local people. From then on, the Gülen movement takes root in that community by building trust with the local community and through both relational and non-relational channels (e.g., joint events, field trips to other Gülen-inspired schools, and the media). The relational model of McAdam and Rucht's diffusion theory helps us understand how the participants in the Gülen movement establish their initial contacts within an unfamiliar community through interpersonal relations. Once the movement's activists have introduced their vision of education to such local individuals as academics, officials or civic leaders, they seek to transfer the discourse of *hizmet* (serving one's fellow human beings) and all the values and practices embedded in it. The introduction of the *hizmet* discourse of the Gülen movement to the members of the new community happens through such relational and non-relational channels as *sohbets*, *himmet* meetings, field trips, seminars, and media. Unlike the diffusion of social movements which is described in McAdam and Rucht's theory as beginning with relational channels and continuing through non-relational channels, the diffusion of the Gülen movement begins with relational channels and continues through both relational and non-relational channels. In addition, unlike the diffusion of a social movement into a new community through its contact and cooperation with another social movement active in that community, the diffusion of the Gülen movement happens through the contact and cooperation between movement volunteers and individuals in the new community, who neither know each other nor have they been engaged together in a collective action previously.

The diffusion of the Gülen movement into a community means simply the adoption of the movement's *hizmet* discourse by the local individuals. In proportion to the level of their adoption of the values and ideas introduced with the discourse, the individuals conduct the practices commonly found in the movement as well. The *hizmet* discourse introduces to the individuals two sets of concepts: theoretical and operational/structural. The theoretical concepts include *gaye-i hayal* (one's purpose of life), *diğergamlık* (altruism) with *başkası için yaşama* (living for others), and *mes'uliyet duygusu* (sense of personal responsibility) with *adanmışlık ruhu* (spirit of devotion). Fethullah Gülen himself attributes the utmost importance to these concepts and considers them *sine qua non* attributes of a person of *hizmet*. The operational/structural concepts include *sohbet* (conversation), *istişare* (collective decision making), *mütevelli* (board of trustees), and *himmet* (personal commitment) and *verme tutkusu* (passion for giving). These are the concepts that describe the practices which an individual becomes involved with as he or she exercises the theoretical concepts of the *hizmet* discourse of the Gülen movement.

The diffusion of the Gülen movement into the city of Mardin, arguably representative of a majority of the countries, regions or continents in which the movement has been active with its schools and cultural activities, illustrates how local individuals mobilize in the movement and adopt the discourse of *hizmet*. Mardin has a population with diverse ethno-religious identities, including Turks, Kurds, Arabs, and Assyrian Christians. Despite the fact that these ethnic communities have not engaged in any visible conflict with one another as communities, they have lived in their own enclaves within the borders of Mardin. In addition to ethno-religious diversity, the city has had a bitter experience of clashes among the Turkish security forces, the PKK (which utilizes the discourse of Kurdish nationalism), and Hizbullah (which uses a radical Islamist discourse). In addition to security problems, the city has suffered from economic underdevelopment, high unemployment, and shortages in the field of education in terms of both infrastructure and educators. These socio-economic and security characteristics are common at varying levels in the vast majority of the countries in which the movement has been active.

The diffusion into Mardin started in the late 1980s with one young man's frequent conversation meetings with a local individual. The conversations, where the two discussed the chronic problems of the Mardin community, such as the absence of sufficient educational facilities and teachers, unemployment, and insecurity caused by the PKK and the Hizbullah, gradually attracted more and more individuals. The young man's introduction of the educational vision of the Gülen movement to that growing number of individuals in Mardin initiated the diffusion of the movement into the city. The ensuing *sohbet* meetings and the field trips to cities where the educational vision of the movement had been put into practice encouraged the Mardinian individuals to adopt the movement's *hizmet* discourse. Consequently, those individuals in Mardin have fulfilled the educational vision of Gülen and the movement by establishing such educational facilities as university preparatory courses, a private school, reading halls, and community service institutions.

APPENDIX

Photographs

1.The city of Mardin

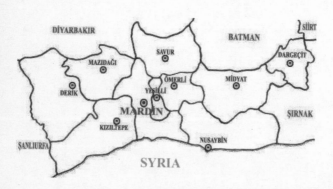

2. Mardin is on Turkey's border with Syria.

3. A demonstration against terrorism

4. Destruction due to terrorist activity

5. A PKK demonstration for Kurdish separatism

6. A Hizbullah banner is displayed.

7. Outside view of local state school

8. The entrance to a local state primary school

9. The environment in local state schools is poor.

10. Fathers carry their daughters through a swollen stream to school.

11. Outside view of Atak Koleji

12. Atak Koleji computer laboratory

13. Some of Atak Koleji's sports facilities

14. Display of children's work in Atak Koleji

15. Atak Koleji's chess club

16. Atak students participate in drama activities.

17. Local people visit the school fair.

18. Visitors view students' artwork at Atak Koleji's annual fair.

19. The "Twenty Minutes' Reading a Day" program

20. Local women attend literacy classes in Atak Koleji.

21. Parents receive awards for reading.

22. There are frequent teacher-parent meetings.

23. The school holds frequent dinner events.

24. SUR students in a lesson
25. Outside view of SUR university preparatory course premises

26. MARKOYDER outreach to parents in rural areas

27. MARKOYDER and teachers encourage parents to send girls and boys to school.

28. The tradition of not sending girls to school is rapidly changing.

29. Environmental conservation activity organized by MARKOYDER

30. Headquarters of MOSDER

31. MOSDER's reading halls build rural children's enthusiasm for education.

32. MOSDER has a reading hall in Dargeçit, the most deprived province of Mardin.

33. The building rented to be the reading hall.

34. Students doing independent study in Dargeçit's reading hall.

35. Record of borrowing in one of MOSDER's reading halls.

NOTES

1   It is necessary from the outset to distinguish between Hizbullah in Mardin and Hizbullah in Lebanon. According to the local people, Hizbullah, or "Hizbul Contra" as they put it, was a counter-guerilla organization set up by the state to oppose the PKK in southeastern Turkey. The local people say "Hizbul Contra" instead of "Hizbul Allah," since, in their words, an organization that has any sort of attachment to Allah cannot undertake such killings.

2   For a short list of Gülen's speeches, see http://tr.fgulen.com/a.page/kasetleri/konferanslar/c38.html (accessed May 20, 2006).

3   In an article titled "Gülen'in Eğitim İmparatorluğu," *Yeni Aktuel* (November 10, 2005), it is argued that the schools associated with the Gülen movement are operating in ninety-one different countries. The article also provides a definitive list of the countries in which they operate.

4   Recently, there has been speculation about the status of the Gülen-inspired schools in Russia. Several newspapers in Turkey, such as *Hürriyet, Milliyet,* and *Cumhuriyet* reported that these have been shut down by the Russian government. However, the Turkish embassy in Moscow has disputed this allegation by responding that none of these schools in Russia has been shut down and that they are operating as normal. See "Büyüklelcilik: 'Türk okulları kapatıldı' haberleri yalan," *Zaman* (February 15, 2006), http://www.zaman.com.tr/ihn=256360&bl=haberler&trh=20060215 (accessed March 6, 2006).

5   Sidney Griffith and Zeki Sarıtoprak, "Fethullah Gülen and the 'People of the Book': A Voice from Turkey for Interfaith Dialogue," *The Muslim World* 95, no. 3 (July 2005): 335.

6   Ibid., 333.

7   Ibid., 337.

8   Lester Kurtz, "Gülen's Paradox: Combining Commitment and Tolerance," *The Muslim World* 95, no. 3 (July 2005): 378.

9   Ahmet Kuru, "Fethullah Gülen's Search for a Middle Way between Modernity and Muslim Tradition," in M. Hakan Yavuz and John L. Esposito, eds., *Turkish Islam and the Secular State: The Gülen Movement* (Syracuse: Syracuse University Press, 2003), 117.

10 Ibid., 117.

11 M. Fethullah Gülen, *Prophet Muhammad: The Infinite Light*. (London: Truestar, 1995): 200–201; cited in Kuru, "Fethullah Gülen's Search for a Middle Way."

12 Thomas Michel, "Sufism and Modernity in the Thought of Fethullah Gülen," *The Muslim World* 95, no. 3 (July 2005): 349.

[13] Cited in ibid., 350.

[14] Osman Bakar, "Gülen on Religion and Science: A Theological Perspective," *The Muslim World* 95, no. 3 (July 2005): 363.

[15] Fethullah Gülen, *Understanding and Belief: The Essentials of Islamic Faith* (Izmir: Kaynak Yayınları, 1997): 309; cited in Bakar, "Gülen on Religion and Science," 362.

[16] Bakar, "Gülen on Religion and Science," 363.

[17] Fethullah Gülen, *Towards the Lost Paradise* (London: Truestar, 1996), 12; cited in Thomas Michel, "Fethullah Gülen as Educator," in *Turkish Islam and the Secular State,* eds. Yavuz and Esposito, 72.

[18] Michel, "Fethullah Gülen as Educator," 77.

[19] Bekim Agai, "The Gülen Movement's Islamic Ethic of Education," in *Turkish Islam and the Secular State,* eds. Yavuz and Esposito, 50.

[20] Berna Turam, "National Loyalties and International Undertakings: The Case of the Gülen Community in Kazakhstan," in ibid., 192.

[21] Doug McAdam and Dieter Rucht, "The Cross-National Diffusion of Movement Ideas," *Annals of the American Academy of Political and Social Science*, vol. 528, "Citizens, Protest, and Democracy" (July 1993): 63.

[22] Ibid., 58. For more information on the diffusion of new techniques and practices in science, see Everett M. Rogers, *Diffusion of Innovations* (London: Collier Macmillan, 1983).

[23] Elihu Katz, "Diffusion (Interpersonal Influence)." In *International Encyclopedia of the Social Sciences,* ed. David L. Shils (London: Macmillan and Free Press, 1968): 81.

[24] McAdam and Rucht, "Cross-National Diffusion," 59; also see David Strang and John W. Meyer, "Institutional Conditions for Diffusion" (Paper delivered at the Workshop on New Institutional Theory, Ithaca, NY, Nov. 1991); cited by McAdam and Rucht, "Cross-National Diffusion."

[25] For a social movement, such behavior seems unusual. Normally, participants in a social movement would tend to avoid official scrutiny as much as possible. Yet, this unusual behavior seems to benefit the movement by pre-empting possible official suspicion about its intentions. At the public level, such behavior actually demonstrates the legality of the movement's activities. In Mardin, I have observed that movement participants go out of their way to invite such local officials as the mayor, the governor, and the police chief to their institutions on a frequent basis.

[26] M. Fethullah Gülen, "İdealsiz Nesiller" (Generations without Ideals), in *Buhranlar Anaforunda İnsan* (Izmir: Nil Yayınları, 1998), 85.

[27] M. Fethullah Gülen, "Ideal Generations," in *The Statue of Our Souls* (New Jersey: The Light Inc., 2005), 125.

28 Michel, "Fethullah Gülen as Educator," 70.

29 Ali Ünal, *M. Fethullah Gülen: Bir Portre Denemesi* (Istanbul: Nil, 2002), 484.

30 It is difficult to define this segment of Turkish society, which has arduously opposed everything Gülen and the movement have done. The concept of "secular" is not the appropriate word for them because a sizeable part of Turkish society, which both approves of Gülen's vision and supports the relevant education activities either verbally or with their donations, identify themselves as "secular." In addition, the Gülen-inspired schools have been running in secular states since the early 1990s. So, it is important not to view supporting Gülen's vision and being secular as mutually exclusive. Perhaps "militantly secular" or "laicist" would be more suited than "ultra-secular."

31 A recent example of such statements can be found on an audio-recording available at www.herkul.org/bamteli/ (accessed February 18, 2006).

32 In an op-ed piece titled, "Diyalog Zorluğu," *Milliyet* (November 3, 1997), Melih Aşık describes the resistance from both radical secularist and Islamist groups toward the movement's dialogue efforts in Turkey. www.milliyet.com.tr/1997/03/11/yazar/asik.html (accessed April 7, 2006).

33 Excerpt from the author's interview with Cengiz Aydoğdu, head of the Civil Society Organizations and of the Mesopotamia Journalists Association in Kızıltepe-Mardin, on February 9, 2006, in Kızıltepe-Mardin.

34 Excerpt from the author's interview with Ziya Ayhan, a senior member of the Small and Medium Business Association in Kızıltepe-Mardin, on February 9, 2006, in Kızıltepe-Mardin.

35 Excerpt from the author's interview with Ahmet Yusuf on January 31, 2006, in Istanbul.

36 Fethullah Gülen, "Ruh'un Zaferi," *Sızıntı* (July 1983): 383.

37 M. Fethullah Gülen, *Ölçü veya Yoldaki Işıklar* (Istanbul: Nil Yayınları, 1985): 208; cited in Ünal. *M. Fethullah Gülen,* 211.

38 M. Enes Ergene, *Gülen Hareketinin Analizi: Geleneğin Modern Çağa Tanıklığı* (Istanbul: Yeni Akademi Yayınları, 2005), 373.

39 M. Fethullah Gülen, *Yitirilmiş Cennete Doğru* (Istanbul: Nil Yayınları, 1988), 128; cited in Ergene, *Gülen Hareketinin Analizi,* 374.

40 M. Fethullah Gülen, *Işığın Göründüğü Ufuk* (Istanbul: Nil Yayınları, 2000), 194.

41 See Qur'an 50:25; cited in Ergene, *Gülen Hareketinin Analizi,* 338.

42 M. Fethullah Gülen. "Yaşatma İdeali" (The Ideal of Living to Let Live), http://tr.fgulen.com/a.page/eserleri/kendi.dunyamiza.dogru/a4594.html (accessed March 4, 2006).

43 Ibid.

44 M. Fethullah Gülen, "Bir Gönül İnsanı Portresi" (Portrait of a Person of Heart), *Sızıntı,* Cilt 22, Sayi 259 (Ekim 2000); also available in Turkish at

http://tr.fgulen.com/a.page/eserleri/cag.ve.nesil.serisi/ornekleri.kendinden.bir.h areket/a1694.html (accessed March 4, 2006).

45   Qur'an 2:56, 22:7, 6:36.

46   M. Fethullah Gülen. *Yeni Türkiye* 15 (1997): 688; cited in Ünal, *M. Fethullah Gülen,* 267.

47   M. Fethullah Gülen, "Okullar Kapanıyor mu?" *Bamteli.* Audio file in Turkish available at www.herkul.org (accessed March 31, 2006).

48   M. Fethullah Gülen, *Örnekleri Kendinden Bir Hareket* (Istanbul: Nil Yayınları, 2005), 37.

49   See "Adanmışlık Ruhu Çok Önemlidir," in *Fethullah Gülen'le 11 Gün,* ed. Mehmet Gündem (Istanbul: Alfa Press, 2005), 221.

50   Excerpt from my conversation with Fethullah Gülen in Pennsylvania on March 31, 2006.

51   Excerpt from my interview with Vahit Atak in Istanbul on January 28, 2006.

52   Gülen, "Bir Gönül İnsanı Portresi" (accessed March 4, 2006).

53   Ibid.

54   "Küçük Lügat," www.risaleinurenstitusu.org/index.asp (accessed April 4, 2006).

55   I attended the *sohbet* meeting with the health-care workers on the evening of February 5, 2006, and had a chance to interview them in Mardin.

56   This information is based on my observations during the *sohbet* meeting I attended in Nusaybin, Mardin, on February 8, 2006.

57   The Hizbullah in Turkey is not to be confused with the group in Lebanon of the same name but otherwise unconnected.

58   Excerpt from my interview with the respondent in Kızıltepe, Mardin, on February 9, 2006.

59   This information is based on a report from a local Mardinian who is related to these religious schools and seems to be fond of Hizbullah.

60   M. Fethullah Gülen, *The Statue of Our Souls,* (New Jersey: The Light Inc., 2005), 44.

61   Excerpt from my interview with Fatih Asılsoy in Mardin on February 5, 2006.

62   Excerpt from my interview with Davut Bey in Mardin on February 7, 2006.

63   This behavior is visible in the development of the movement in Mardin. Despite the fact that there were other movements in Mardin prior to the Gülen movement, according to my respondents, the movement volunteers have not associated with any of them. Rather, they have sought to communicate with individuals and build their own movement and institutions.

64   Excerpt from my interview with Fatih Asılsoy in Mardin on February 5, 2006.

65   See Latif Erdoğan, *Küçük Dünyam* (Istanbul: Milliyet Yayınları, 1995), 57.

66   For a definitive account of different religious groups in Turkey, see Niyazi Öktem, "Religion in Turkey," *Brigham Young University Law Review* (January 2002): 371–403.

67   See note 1.

68   Excerpt from my interview with the Imam Abdulbari in Nusaybin, Mardin, on February 9, 2006.

69   Excerpt from my interview with Murat Salim in Nusaybin, Mardin, on February 9, 2006.

70   The concept of *sohbet* has a rather more technical and deeper meaning than a mere "weekly tea conversation." I have tried to articulate its meaning in chapter 3. However, throughout the following chapters, I use *sohbet* as it is understood by the people participating in these meetings.

71   Most of the Mardinians I talked to have cited unemployment and lack of education as the main reasons that make it easy for both the PKK and Hizbullah to recruit the youth in Mardin, especially in the rural areas dominated by the Kurds.

72   See www.fatihkoleji.com/tarihce.php and www.yamanlar.k12.com.tr for Fatih High School and Yamanlar High School, respectively (accessed March 16, 2006).

73   For the list of the awards, see www.fatihkoleji.com/olimpiyat_butun.php (accessed March 16, 2006).

74   During my interviews with Vahit Atak (who sponsored the construction of Atak Koleji) and the other Mardinians who have been actively involved in the school projects, all of them stated that the state could not provide the necessary educational facilities in their city.

75   Excerpt from my interview with Hasan Doğru on March 9, 2006.

76   In Turkey, every high school graduate has to pass the university entrance exam to attend university. Mardin was one of the least successful cities in Turkey in terms of its graduates passing this exam.

77   Gülen articulated the tenets of the *hizmet* (serving one's fellows) culture in a series of public conferences titled "İnsanı Yücelten Vasıflar" (Values That Dignify People) between April 9 and November 15, 1989; see http://tr.fgulen.com/a.page/kasetleri/a3707.html (accessed March 16, 2006).

78   Excerpt from my interview with Hayri Bey in Mardin on February 7, 2006.

79   Excerpt from my interview with Davut Bey in Mardin on February 7, 2006.

80   Excerpt from my interview with Fatih Asılsoy in Mardin on February 5, 2006.

81   Excerpt from my interview with Erhan Bey in Mardin on February 4, 2006.

82   Excerpt from my interview with Fatih Asılsoy in Mardin on February 4, 2006.

83   Ibid.

84 Upper Mardin is also called Old Mardin. The city was historically centered at the outskirts of Mardin hill, also the site of Mardin castle.

85 Excerpt from my interview with Fatih Asılsoy in Mardin on February 5, 2006.

86 Excerpt from my interview with Fatih Asılsoy in Mardin on February 5, 2006.

87 Excerpt from my interview with Davut Bey in Mardin on February 7, 2006.

88 Excerpt from my interview with Fatih Asılsoy in Mardin on February 5, 2006.

89 All of my respondents who were the members of Mardin's first *sohbet* group mentioned this incident during my separate interviews with each of them.

90 Excerpt from my interview with Davut Bey in Mardin on February 7, 2006. In fact, all of my respondents mentioned this incident as well.

91 Cihan Sancar is the mayor of Kızıltepe, a county with a population of 200,000 people. It is the center of Kurdish nationalism and the stronghold of the PKK. She is a member of DEHAP, the far-left party that is publicly known as the PKK's political extension.

92 Excerpt from my interview with Orhan Tutkun in Mardin on February 11, 2006.

93 One of the most persistent speculations about the schools' funding has been that they are funded by the CIA. Alternatively, ultra-secular groups in Turkey have argued that the movement is funded by such Islamic states as Iran and Saudi Arabia. The fact that both states declined the movement's request to open schools counters this accusation. The most prominent critic of the movement in the Turkish media has been the columnist Hikmet Çetinkaya of the daily *Cumhuriyet*. See "Fethullah Gülen," www.islamiyetgercekleri.org/fethullahgulen.html (accessed March 28, 2006).

94 Excerpt from my interview with Fatih Asılsoy in Mardin on February 5, 2006.

95 Gülen's public address, "Gönül Dünyamızdan I," was delivered in the city of Afyon on June 27, 1980, and is one of the early examples of when he mentioned the sacrifices of Abu Bakr and Omar while defining the concept of *fedakarlık* (sacrifice) and *diğergamlık* (altruism).

96 The names of these two men were frequently mentioned by movement participants during my interviews with them. Mr. Erimez owned large pieces of land including hills that had olive trees; hence the title.

97 See "Kendini Gençlere Adayan Bir İnsan: Hacı Kemal Erimez" (trans: A Man who Dedicated his Life to Young People), http://ailem.zaman.com.tr/ibl=26&hn=4360 (accessed March 16, 2006).

98 Excerpt from my interview with Mehmet Ali Şengül in Pennsylvania on February 12, 2006.

99 Excerpt from my conversation with Fethullah Gülen in Pennsylvania on February 11, 2006.

¹⁰⁰ Orhan Tutkun, a senior administrator in the Gülen-inspired schools in Mardin, noted that every teacher in those institutions meets the monthly expenses of at least one secondary or high school student.

¹⁰¹ Excerpt from my interview with Hadji Burhan in Midyat-Mardin on February 7, 2006.

¹⁰² The first *himmet* meeting took place during spring 1992. Excerpt from my interview with Hadji Burhan in Midyat-Mardin on February 7, 2006.

¹⁰³ Excerpt from my interview with Fatih Asılsoy in Mardin on February 5, 2006.

¹⁰⁴ Excerpt from my interview with Erhan Bey in Mardin on February 4, 2006.

¹⁰⁵ Excerpt from my interview with Orhan Tutkun in Mardin on February 10, 2006.

¹⁰⁶ Excerpt from my interview with Vahit Atak, the businessman who funded the construction of Mardin's Atak High School, in Istanbul on January 28, 2006.

¹⁰⁷ I attended an *istişare* (collective decision making) meeting in Mardin. The local people and teachers at the school were discussing such issues as upcoming cultural activities, opening a new reading hall in Savur, and constructing a second university preparatory course in Mardin. They hold these meetings every other week.

¹⁰⁸ Excerpt from my interview with Hayri Bey in Mardin on February 7, 2006.

¹⁰⁹ By 1996, the number of *sohbet* groups had already increased. I will examine the proliferation of these groups in a later section.

¹¹⁰ Excerpt from my interview with Fatih Asılsoy in Mardin on February 7, 2006.

¹¹¹ Excerpt from my interview with Fatih Asılsoy and Hayri Bey in Mardin on February 5, 2006.

¹¹² I owe this insightful comment, along with many others, to my thesis advisor Dr. Charles King, Government Department, Georgetown University.

¹¹³ Excerpt from my interview with Fatih Asılsoy in Mardin on February 7, 2006. This information was confirmed by all of my inteviewees. The Atak family is from Mardin and, as Vahit Atak explains, moved to Istanbul in 1974 because of local socio-economic deprivation and security problems.

¹¹⁴ Excerpt from my interview with Vahit Atak in Istanbul on January 28, 2006.

¹¹⁵ The actual analogy was made by Ibrahim Bey during that meeting, as confirmed by both Vahit Atak and the participants with whom I spoke. I think it is useful to put it here in order to better understand the philosophy behind the movement's education campaign.

¹¹⁶ Excerpt from my interview with Vahit Atak in Istanbul on January 28, 2006.

¹¹⁷ It is important to note that even though the movement has been essentially a civic education movement, as it has achieved a global reach and become active in societies with different religions, races, cultures, and languages, its second

most emphasized theme has, perhaps, been the need for intercultural dialogue. While the movement was still only in Turkey, this dialogue was intra-cultural. So, the movement has used its education campaign to help build bridges between different social segments in Turkey first and then in other societies.

[118] Excerpt from my interview with Vahit Atak in Istanbul on January 28, 2006.

[119] The event took place in the evening of February 5, 2006.

[120] Excerpt from my interview with Murat Bey in Kızıltepe-Mardin on February 6, 2006.

[121] The Mardin case does not answer the question of whether men and women hold events together or separately because such mixed gatherings are not normal in the culture of the city. However, in other encounters with the activities of the movement in such cities as Istanbul, Ankara, and Trabzon, I saw that men and women held events together.

[122] With regards to both men's and women's activities, my respondents reported that Assyrians participate in the education projects in Mardin and that several of their children attend Atak High School. The absence of the Yezidis is, to a great extent, due to the fact that they mostly live in the rural areas and are a small group.

[123] Excerpt from my interview with the respondent in Mardin on February 10, 2006.

[124] Excerpt from my interview with the respondent in Mardin on February 10, 2006.

[125] Excerpt from my interview with the respondent in Mardin on February 10, 2006.

[126] I obtained this information through my interviews with the local people who helped the movement open its first university preparatory course in Mardin in 1992.

[127] Excerpt from my interview with Murat Salim on February 9, 2006, in Nusaybin, Mardin.

[128] Excerpt from my interview with Murat Salim on February 9, 2006 in Nusaybin, Mardin.

[129] Excerpt from my interview with Fatih Asılsoy on February 6, 2006, in Mardin.

[130] These are the moral values that Gülen introduced in the *hizmet* discourse. See chapter 2, "The *Hizmet* Discourse of the Gülen Movement."

[131] Excerpt from my interview with the respondent on February 8, 2006, in Nusaybin.

[132] See chapter 4, "Emergence and Development in Mardin."

[133] This information is based on my interview with the Atak Koleji teachers on February 3, 2006, in Mardin. Several other respondents of both Kurdish and Arab origin confirmed this information at different times and places.

[134] This information is based on my notes from my trip to Atak Koleji on February 3, 2006.

[135] These are the most notable private schools associated with the movement and the best known ones because of their success in the international science contests.

[136] Excerpt from my interview with Oğuz Ozan at Atak Koleji on February 3, 2006.

[137] The principal reported that fifteen percent of the students are granted scholarships according to their performance on the scholarship test held at the beginning of the school year.

[138] Excerpt from my interview with a groups of women from Surgucu village on February 2, 2006.

[139] Excerpt from my interview with Hayri Serhat on February 9, 2006 in Kızıltepe, Mardin.

[140] I did not obtain specific figures for either the general literacy rate or for the female literacy rate. However, my respondents confirmed these facts.

[141] At different times and places, several people that I interviewed used the same term to refer to the school's large number of public events held throughout the year.

[142] This information is based on my interview with Şükrü Bey on February 11, 2006, in Dargeçit, Mardin.

[143] Excerpt from my interview with Imam Abdulbari on February 9, 2006, in Nusaybin, Mardin.

[144] Excerpt from my interview with Oğuz Ozan at Atak Koleji on February 3, 2006.

BIBLIOGRAPHY

INTERVIEWS

Disclaimer: The names of some of my interviewees have been changed in order to protect their confidentiality. Interviews are listed in chronological order.

Vahit Atak, Mardinian businessman and donor to the Gülen-inspired institutions in Istanbul; January 28, 2006.

Malik Bey, teacher and former coordinator of the Gülen-inspired schools in Mardin; January 31, 2006.

Parents in Surgucu village whose children attend the Gülen-inspired schools in Mardin; February 3, 2006.

Muhtar (administrator) of Pinardere village; February 3, 2006.

Oğuz Ozan, teacher and principal in a Gülen-inspired school; February 3, 2006.

Fatih Asılsoy, local businessman and donor to the activities of the movement in Mardin; February 4–5, 2006.

Harun Tanrikulu, local businessman who has recently become involved with the movement in Mardin; February 4, 2006.

Erhan Bey, local businessman and donor to the activities of the movement in Mardin; February 4, 2006.

Fethi Bey, senior member of the Mardin Village Development Association; February 4, 2006.

Hayri Bey, local businessman and donor to the activities of the movement in Mardin; February 5, 2006.

Female students at Sur Dersanesi (university preparatory course) in Kızıltepe, Mardin; February 6, 2006.

Davut Karaman, an *aşiret* (clan) leader in Kızıltepe, Mardin; February 6, 2006.

Serafettin Ağa, an *aşiret* (clan) leader in Kızıltepe, Mardin; February 6, 2006.

Male students at Sur Dersanesi (university preparatory course) in Kızıltepe, Mardin; February 6, 2006.

Cihan Sancar, mayor of Kızıltepe, Mardin; February 6, 2006.

Hadji Burhan, local senior citizen who has been actively involved with the movement in Midyat, Mardin; February 7, 2006.

İsa Gülten, assistant to the Assyrian Christian Metropolitan in Midyat, Mardin; February 7, 2006.

Samuel Aktaş, the Assyrian Christian Metropolitan in Midyat, Mardin; February 7, 2006.

Hüseyin Adem, mayor of Midyat, Mardin; February 7, 2006.

Imam Abdulbari, imam in Nusaybin, Mardin; February 9, 2006.

Abdulkadir Bey, editor-in-chief of a local newspaper in Nusaybin, Mardin; February 9, 2006.

Hadji Arif, former member of the political party that sympathizes with the PKK in Nusaybin, Mardin; February 9, 2006.

Murat Salim, local businessman who has recently become involved with the movement in Nusaybin, Mardin; February 9, 2006.

Murat Okçu, senior reporter in a local newspaper in Nusaybin, Mardin; February 9, 2006.

Cengiz Aydoğdu, senior member of the Mesopotamia Journalists Association in Kızıltepe, Mardin; February 9, 2006.

Hayri Serhat, local businessman and father of two children attending the Gülen-inspired school in Mardin; February 9, 2006.

Fettah Arslan, local businessman and sponsor of the Gülen-inspired schools in Mardin; February 9, 2006.

Seyda Ahmet, local sheikh in Kızıltepe, Mardin; February 9, 2006.

Ziya Ayhan, senior member of the small business association in Kızıltepe, Mardin; February 9, 2006.

İsa Tunc, senior member of the local businessmen's association in Kızıltepe, Mardin; February 9, 2006.

Muhtar (administrator) of Dara village; February 9, 2006.

Mahir Mardini, an *aşiret* (clan) leader in Kızıltepe, Mardin; February 10, 2006.

Orhan Tutkun, senior administrator in the Gülen-inspired schools in Mardin; February 10, 2006.

Murat Kolda, an Assyrian businessman in Mardin; February 11, 2006.

PRIMARY SOURCES

Gülen, M. Fethullah, *Fasıldan Fasıla*, 4 vols., 7th ed. Izmir: Nil, 1995.

————, *Kur'ân ve Sünnet Perspektifinde Kader* (Destiny from the Perspective of the Qur'an and the Sunna). Izmir: Isik Yayınları, 1995.

————, *İnancın Gölgesinde* (In the Shadow of Faith), 2 vols. Izmir: Nil Yayınları, 1996.

————, *Prophet Muhammad as Commander*. London: Truestar, 1996.

————, *Toward the Lost Paradise*. London: Truestar, 1996.

————, *Asrın Getirdiği Tereddütler* (The Questions Posed by Our Century), 4 vols., 11th ed. Izmir: T.O.V., 1997.

————, *Buhranlar Anaforunda İnsan* (*Çağ ve Nesil* 2) (The Human in the Whirlpool of Crisis), 11th ed. Izmir: T.O.V., 1997.

————, *Kalbin Zümrüt Tepeleri* (The Emerald Hills of the Heart). Izmir: Nil, 1997.

————, *Prizma* (Prism), 3 vols. Istanbul: Zaman, 1997.

————, *Understanding and Belief: The Essentials of the Islamic Faith*, tr. Ali Ünal. Izmir: Kaynak, 1997.

————, *Yeşeren Düşünceler* (*Çağ ve Nesil* 6) (Growing Thoughts), 2nd ed. Izmir: T.O.V., 1997.

————, *Zamanın Altın Dilimi* (*Çağ ve Nesil* 4) (The Golden Piece of Time), 10th ed. Izmir: T.O.V., 1997.

————, *Fatiha Üzerine Mülahazalar* (Some Reflections on the Fatiha: Qur'an Chapter 1). Izmir: Nil, 1998.

————, *İrşad Ekseni* (The Axis of Guidance). Izmir: Zaman, 1998.

————, *Ölçü veya Yoldaki Işıklar* (Criteria or the Lights of the Way), 4 vols. Izmir: Nil, 1998.

————, *Ölüm Ötesi Hayat* (Life after Death). Izmir: Nil, 1998.

————, *Ruhumuzun Heykelini Dikerken* (The Statue of Our Souls). Izmir: Nil, 1998.

————, *Varlığın Metafizik Boyutu* (The Metaphysical Dimension of Existence), 2 vols. Izmir: Nil, 1998.

————, *Key Concepts in the Practice of Sufism: The Emerald Hills of the Heart,* 2 vols., tr. Ali Ünal. Fairfax, VA: Fountain, 1999.

————, *Çocuk Terbiyesi* (Child Education). Izmir: Nil, 2000.

————, *Işığın Göründüğü Ufuk* (The Horizon of Light). Izmir: Nil, 2000.

————, *Kırık Mızrap* (The Broken Plectrum), 2 vols. Izmir: Nil, 2000.

————, *Kur'ân'dan İdrake Yansıyanlar* (Reflections from the Qur'an on Our Understanding). Istanbul: Zaman, 2000.

————, *Pearls of Wisdom.* Fairfax, VA: Fountain, 2000.

————, *Prophet Muhammad: Aspects of His Life,* 2 vols., tr. Ali Ünal. Fairfax, VA: Fountain, 2000.

————, "A Comparative Approach to Islam and Democracy." *SAIS Review* 21, no.2 (Summer–Fall 2001): 133–38.

————, *Toward a Global Civilization of Love and Tolerance.* New Jersey: The Light, Inc., 2004.

————, *Statue of Our Souls: Revival in Islamic Thought and Activism,* tr. Muhammed Çetin. New Jersey: The Light, Inc., 2005.

SECONDARY SOURCES

Agai, Bekim. "The Gülen Movement's Islamic Ethic of Education." In *Turkish Islam and the Secular State: The Gülen Movement*, edited by M. Hakan Yavuz and John L. Esposito, 48–68. Syracuse: Syracuse University Press, 2003.

Altinoglu, Ebru. *Fethullah Gülen's Perception of State and Society.* Istanbul: Bosphorus University, 1999.

Aras, Bulent. "Turkish Islam's Moderate Face." *Middle East Quarterly* 5, no. 3 (September 1998): 23–30.

Aras, Bulent and Omer Caha. "Fethullah Gülen and His Liberal 'Turkish Islam' Movement." *Middle East Review of International Affairs Journal* 4, no. 4 (December 2000): 30–42.

Balci, Bayram. "Fethullah Gülen's Missionary Schools in Central Asia and Their Role in the Spreading of Turkism and Islam." *Religion, State & Society* 31, no. 2 (2003): 151–77.

Bakar, Osman. "Gülen on Religion and Science: A Theological Perspective." *The Muslim World* 95, no. 3 (July 2005): 359–72.

Eickelman, F. Dale. "Inside the Islamic Reformation." *Wilson Quarterly* 22, no. 1 (Winter 1998): 84–85.

Ergene, M. Enes. *Gülen Hareketinin Analizi: Geleneğin Modern Çağa Tanıklığı.* Istanbul: Yeni Akademi Yayınları, 2005.

Gündem, Mehmet. *Fethullah Gülen'le 11 Gün.* Istanbul: Alfa Press, 2005.

Katz, Elihu. "Diffusion (Interpersonal Influence)." In *International Encyclopedia of the Social Sciences*, edited by David L. Shils, 78–85. London: Macmillan and Free Press, 1968.

Kosebalaban, Hasan. "The Making of Enemy and Friend: Fethullah Gülen's National Security Identity." In *Turkish Islam and the Secular State: The Gülen Movement*, edited by M. Hakan Yavuz and John L. Esposito, 170–83. Syracuse: Syracuse University Press, 2003.

Kurtz, R. Lester. "Gülen's Paradox: Combining Commitment and Tolerance." *The Muslim World* 95, no. 3 (July 2005): 373–84.

Kuru, Ahmet. "Globalization and Diversification of Islamic Movements: Three Turkish Cases." *Political Science Quarterly* (Summer 2005): 253–74.

————. "Fethullah Gülen's Search for a Middle Way between Modernity and Tradition: The Case of Fethullah Gülen." In

Turkish Islam and the Secular State: The Gülen Movement, edited by M. Hakan Yavuz and John L. Esposito, 115–30. Syracuse: Syracuse University Press, 2003.

McAdam, Doug and Dieter Rucht. "The Cross-National Diffusion of Movement Ideas," *Annals of the American Academy of Political and Social Science* 528, Citizens, Protest, and Democracy (July 1993): 56–74.

Michel, Thomas. "Two Frontrunners for Peace: John Paul II and Fethullah Gülen." Unpublished paper presented at the Front Runners for Peace Symposia. Organized by the Cosmicus Foundation on March 16–18, 2004, in Amsterdam, Holland.

———. "Sufism and Modernity in the Thought of Fethullah Gülen." *The Muslim World* 95, no. 3 (July 2005): 341–58.

———. "Fethullah Gülen as Educator." In *Turkish Islam and the Secular State: The Gülen Movement*, edited by M. Hakan Yavuz and John L. Esposito, 69–84. Syracuse: Syracuse University Press, 2003.

Öktem, Niyazi. "Religion in Turkey." *Brigham Young University Law Review* (January 2002): 371–403.

Özdalga, Elisabeth. "Following in the Footsteps of Fethullah Gülen: Three Woman Teachers Tell Their Stories." In *Turkish Islam and the Secular State: The Gülen Movement*, 85–114, edited by M. Hakan Yavuz and John L. Esposito. Syracuse: Syracuse University Press, 2003.

———. "Redeemer or Outsider? The Gülen Community in the Civilizing Process." *The Muslim World* 95, no. 3 (July 2005): 429–46.

———. "Entrepreneurs with a Mission: Turkish Islamists Building Schools along the Silk Road." Unpublished paper delivered at the Annual Conference of the North American Middle East Studies Association, Washington DC (November 19–22, 1999).

———. "Worldly Asceticism in Islamic Casting: Fethullah Gülen's Inspired Piety and Activism." *Critique* 17 (Fall 2000): 83–104.

Sarıtoprak, Zeki. "An Islamic Approach to Peace and Nonviolence: A Turkish Experience." *The Muslim World* 95, no. 3 (July 2005): 413–28.

———. "Fethullah Gülen: A Sufi in His Own Way." Paper delivered at the seminar "Islamic Modernities: Fethullah Gülen and Contemporary Islam," Georgetown University (April 26–27, 2001).

Sarıtoprak, Zeki and Ali Ünal. "An Interview with Fethullah Gülen." *The Muslim World* 95, no. 3 (July 2005): 447–68.

Sarıtoprak, Zeki and Sidney Griffith. "Fethullah Gülen and the 'People of the Book': A Voice from Turkey for Interfaith Dialogue." *The Muslim World* 95, no. 3 (July 2005): 329–40.

Sevindi, Nevval. *Fethullah Gülen ile New York Sohbeti*. Istanbul: Sabah Yayınları, 1997.

Turam, Berna. *Between Islam and the State: The Politics of Engagement*. Unpublished PhD. dissertation, McGill University, Montreal.

———. "National Loyalties and International Undertakings: The Case of the Gülen Community in Kazakhstan." In *Turkish Islam and the Secular State: The Gülen Movement*, edited by M. Hakan Yavuz and John L. Esposito, 184–207. Syracuse: Syracuse University Press, 2003.

Ünal, Ali. *M. Fethullah Gülen: Bir Portre Denemesi*. Istanbul: Nil, 2002.

Ünal, Kudret. *Medya Aynasında Fethullah Gülen: Kozadan Kelebeğe* (Fethullah Gülen in the Media Mirror: From Cocoon to Butterfly), 1st ed. Istanbul: Gazeteciler ve Yazarlar Vakfı Yayınları, 1999.

Yavuz, M. Hakan. "Search for a New Social Contract in Turkey: Fethullah Gülen, the Virtue Party, and the Kurds." *SAIS Review* 19 (1999): 114–43.

———. "Towards an Islamic Liberalism? The Nurcu Movement and Fethullah Gülen in Turkey." *The Middle East Journal* 53 (1999): 584–605.

University Press, 2003, especially chapter 8, 179–206.

Yavuz, M. Hakan, and John L. Esposito. *Turkish Islam and the Secular State: The Gülen Movement.* Syracuse: Syracuse University Press, 2003.

Yilmaz, Ihsan. "Ijtihad and Tajdid by Conduct: The Gülen Movement." In *Turkish Islam and the Secular State: The Gülen Movement*, edited by M. Hakan Yavuz and John L. Esposito, 208–37. Syracuse: Syracuse University Press, 2003.

———. "State, Law, Civil Society, and Islam in Contemporary Turkey." *The Muslim World* 95, no. 3 (July 2005): 385–413.

INDEX

A

Abu Bakr, 55, 114

activist: -adopters, 14, 42; transmitters, 14, 42

adanmışlık ruhu (spirit of devotion), 19, 29-31, 39

administrator (*muhtar*), 53, 70, 75, 79, 117, 123, 125

adopter, 15, 16, 42, 43

Agai, Bekim, 13, 112

Akif Bey, 49, 50, 51, 52, 54, 57, 59, 70

al-Qaeda, 35, 82

altruism, 19, 21, 24, 31, 33, 34, 38, 39, 66, 89, 114

Ankara, 3, 38, 46, 59, 60, 80, 118

Arabs, viii, 67, 73, 82, 90

armed struggle, 35

Armenian: community, 10

asceticism, 11, 128

Asia-Pacific, 4

Asılsoy, Fatih, 37, 38, 43, 44, 47, 48, 49, 50, 51, 52, 53, 57, 60, 64, 70, 114, 115, 116, 117, 121

Aslandoğan, Alp, xi

Assyrian Christians, viii, 67, 90

Atak family, 61, 63, 72, 115

Atak, Mahmut, 61

Atak Koleji (High School), 30, 67, 68, 72, 73, 74, 75, 76, 77, 78, 79, 80, 81, 82, 83, 84, 98, 99, 100, 101, 102, 115, 116, 117

Atak Restaurant, 79

Atak, Vahit, 30, 58, 61, 62, 63, 65, 115, 121; adopting the *hizmet* discourse, 63

austerity, 27

Australia, 4

Aydoğdu, Cengiz, 23, 111, 122

Ayhan, Ziya, 23, 111, 122

Azerbaijan: first high school abroad, 4

B

Bakar, Osman, 12, 86, 110

Balıkesir, 77

başkası için yaşama (living for others), 19. *See also* altruism

Biblical prophets, 11

blacksmith, 30

board of trustees. *See* mütevelli

Bölükbaşı, İsmail, 60

Buddhist, 6

Buhranlar Anaforunda İnsan, 20, 110, 123

Bulgaria, 4

businessmen, 2, 4, 17, 33, 34, 38, 44, 46, 47, 48, 49, 56, 59, 72, 122; dedication of, 48